JUDGE
FOR YOURSELF

MAO ZEDONG

CHRISTINE HATT

WORLD ALMANAC® LIBRARY

Please visit our web site at: www.worldalmanaclibrary.com
For a free color catalog describing World Almanac® Library's list
of high-quality books and multimedia programs, call 1-800-848-2928 (USA)
or 1-800-387-3178 (Canada). World Almanac® Library's fax: (414) 332-3567.

Library of Congress Cataloging-in-Publication Data

Hatt, Christine.
    Mao Zedong / by Christine Hatt.
       p. cm. — (Judge for yourself)
    Summary: Describes the life of Chinese Communist leader Mao Zedong in the context of the history
of 20th century China and his immense impact on that history.
    Includes index.
    ISBN 0-8368-5536-1 (lib. bdg.)
    1. Mao, Zedong, 1893-1976—Juvenile literature. 2. Heads of state—China—Biography—Juvenile literature.
[1. Mao, Zedong, 1893-1976. 2. Heads of state. 3. China—History—20th century.] I. Title. II. Series.
DS778.M3H374   2003
951.05'092—dc21   2003045005

This North American edition first published in 2004 by
World Almanac® Library
330 West Olive Street, Suite 100
Milwaukee, WI 53212 USA

This U.S. edition copyright © 2004 by World Almanac® Library. Original edition published in Great Britain by
Evans Brothers Limited. Copyright © 2002 by Evans Brothers Limited, 2A Portman Mansions, Chiltern Street,
London W1U 6NR, United Kingdom. This U.S. edition published under license from Evans Brothers Limited.

Consultant: Richard Louis Edmonds
Editor: Jinny Johnson
Design: Mark Holt
Maps: Tim Smith
Production: Jenny Mulvanny
Picture research: Julia Bird
Gareth Stevens editor: Alan Wachtel
Gareth Stevens designer: Scott M. Krall

Photo credits: t–top, c–center, b–bottom, r–right, l–left, David King Collection: Front cover, back cover (top and
bottom), title page, 4t, 5t, 6b, 10, 11b, 15t, 16t, 16b, 17, 26, 30, 34, 35, 36, 37, 38, 39, 41b, 45, 49, 59, Hulton
Getty: 14, 21, 29t, 29b, 31l, 33, 55, 60, Mary Evans Picture Library: Back cover (middle), 7, 8, 15b, 18, 19tc,
19tr, 20, 43, 46, 58, Robert Harding Picture Library: 12, 13t, 13l, 13r, Topham Picturepoint: 6t, 9, 11t, 19b, 23,
25, 28, 31r, 32, 40, 41t, 42, 44, 47, 48, 50, 51, 52, 53, 54, 56, 57, 61

Printed in Canada

1 2 3 4 5 6 7 8 9 07 06 05 04 03

CONTENTS

JUDGE
FOR YOURSELF

INTRODUCTION

Mao Zedong, born the son of a peasant in 1893, rose to become the most important figure in 20th-century China. In the civil war that followed the overthrow of imperial rule in the country, his unique combination of vision, determination, political shrewdness, and military skill played a central role in leading the Communists to victory over the Nationalists. As ruler of China from the foundation of the People's Republic in 1949 until his death in 1976, he also led his country through long years of unparalleled turbulence and tragedy.

This book looks at Mao Zedong and his activities in two ways. The first is the straightforward story of Mao's 82-year life—

In the 1960s, at the height of his power, Mao was cheered by adoring crowds in Beijing.

Red Guards dreamed of seizing Taiwan from their Nationalist opponents.

一定要解放台湾

We are determined to liberate Taiwan!
Nous libérerons Taïwan!
Wir werden Taiwan unbedingt befreien!

CHINESE SPELLING

European translators represent the words of the Chinese language with the letters of the Roman alphabet. There are several ways of doing this, and the best-known English system is called the Wade-Giles, named after its creators. In this system, Mao Zedong's name, for example, is spelled "Mao Tse-tung."

The Chinese, however, developed their own system, known as *pinyin*. In 1979, this system was officially adopted in China, and it is now widely accepted throughout the world. This book uses *pinyin* spellings, with three main exceptions. The Nationalist Party is referred to as the Kuomintang (in pinyin, Guomindang), because this is how its members still spell its name. Wade-Giles names are used for the Nationalist politicians Sun Yat-sen (in pinyin, Sun Yixian) and Chiang Kai-shek (in pinyin, Jiang Jieshi) because the pinyin versions are little known.

毛 泽 东 主 席

Mao's Communists defeated the Nationalists on the Chinese mainland in 1949. Here, a Communist truck rolls through Shanghai.

in other words, his biography. This part is divided into chapters, and it also includes special features that highlight two subjects—China's imperial history and Chinese philosophies—and consider how both affected Mao's thoughts and actions.

The second part of the book examines the main themes of Mao Zedong's adult life—his beliefs, policies, and relationships—more closely. To help you assess his ideals and actions for yourself, this part is divided into sections, each headed with an important question to consider. The first two pages of each section provide one possible answer, together with quotations, statistics, and other facts to back it up. The next two pages provide a second potential answer, also with supporting evidence and information.

The question pages can be used in several ways. You may simply want to read them through, look at both answers and their supporting evidence, and then make up your own mind about which answer is stronger. Perhaps you could also write down the reasons for your decision. Alternatively, the material can be used in a classroom debate between two groups, each arguing for a different answer. The provided sources may also inspire further research. You may wish to use the library or the Internet to find more data to back your answers to the questions on which these pages focus.

The question pages have another purpose. They are designed to show you that facts and statistics can be used to support completely different points of view. This is why historians have to sift through a great deal of material, from a wide variety of sources, before they can reach reliable conclusions about the past. Even then, answers are rarely clear-cut and may be overturned by new evidence. As you consider the questions, remember that neither of the answers provided may be completely correct. Using the information in both parts of the book—and any more you can find—it is up to you to judge for yourself.

CHAPTER ONE

THE EARLY YEARS

The East is Red, the sun rises.
In China a Mao Zedong is born.
He seeks the people's happiness.
He is the people's Great Savior.

This anthem to Mao Zedong was written in the early 1940s, during his rise to power. There was nothing, however, in the circumstances of Mao's birth that suggested he would grow up to be a great man. Mao came into the world on December 26, 1893, a bitter winter day, in the village of Shaoshan in the southern China province of Hunan. He was the

Mao's family home in Shaoshan, surrounded by fertile wooded slopes.

This 1917 family portrait shows Mao (far right), his mother, and his brothers (left).

first child of Mao Rensheng, a soldier turned rice farmer, and Wen Qimei, a gentle woman of deep Buddhist faith but little education. Eventually, Mao shared his parents with two brothers, Zemin and Zetan, and an adopted sister, Zejian.

A FADING EMPIRE

At the time of Mao's birth, China was ruled by Emperor Guangxu, a member of the Qing dynasty. The splendid trappings of Qing power could not disguise the fact that the empire was in decline. Qing rule, which had begun in 1644 and ushered in a period of great prosperity and expansion, was, by the 19th century, corrupt and weak. The Qing emperors had largely turned their back on the industrial growth that was transforming and enriching the West.

FOREIGN INTERFERENCE

Pressure from abroad added to China's internal problems. By the 19th century, Britain, France, the United States, and other Western powers were flourishing as a result of the Industrial Revolution and wanted to increase trade with the Chinese. China's rulers, however, allowed foreign merchants only in the port of Guangzhou (formerly known as Canton). Frustrated by this restriction, Europeans took matters into their own hands. Beginning with the Opium Wars, they used force to increase their trading markets and to take control of territories such as Burma and Vietnam that had previously owed allegiance to China.

In the years immediately after Mao's birth, China's pride suffered another blow. From 1894 to 1895, the country fought and lost a war against Japan. In the aftermath of the war, the Japanese annexed much former Chinese territory, including the island of Taiwan, and demanded payment of a huge fine. Weakened by these losses, China was unable to resist further interference by the European powers and Russia. These foreign countries gradually carved up China into separate "spheres of influence," in which they controlled industry, the railroads, and more.

REFORM AND REBELLION

In 1898, Emperor Guangxu responded to these humiliations by introducing reforms designed to reduce corruption and modernize China's economy and educational system. His efforts were soon crushed by conservative officials and the Dowager Empress Cixi, who stirred up the antiforeigner Boxer Rebellion. The rebellion reached its peak in 1900, when the Boxers seized the embassies in Beijing. After U.S., European, and Japanese troops defeated the rebels, China had to pay another large fine and accept still more foreign intervention.

STARTING SCHOOL

Far away in Hunan province, Mao Zedong was growing up unaware of this turmoil. As a young boy, he helped his father on the farm, and at the age of about eight, he started at the local village school. The teacher was harsh and the learning was by rote. But Mao was a sharp student, and he conscientiously studied the works of Chinese philosophers such as

THE OPIUM WARS

The Chinese emperors of the 18th century had no wish to buy goods from Britain or any other foreign power. But they did allow the British to buy Chinese tea, silk, and porcelain with silver. The British were determined to make the balance of trade more equal, so in the 1780s, they secretly began to send opium from British-ruled India to China. The result was a huge increase in Chinese opium addicts; by the 1830s, there were about 10 million Chinese opium addicts.

Eventually, in 1839, Emperor Daoguang sent a representative to seize the opium stocks in Guangzhou. In response, the British sent in warships, which defeated Chinese troops on the country's coast. British soldiers also seized Shanghai and marched toward Nanjing, leaving the emperor little choice but to accept defeat. In the 1842 Treaty of Nanjing, which ended the war, China agreed to open five new ports to foreigners, give Hong Kong to Britain, and pay a fine of 20 million dollars in silver.

The Second Opium War began in 1858, and the British seized Guangzhou. When the Chinese refused to accept the treaties signed at Tianjin to end the conflict, hostilities flared up again. Finally, in 1860, a joint British and French force marched on Beijing and destroyed the emperor's Summer Palace. China was then forced to accept treaties that gave foreigners yet more influence in the nation.

In this 1841 scene from the First Opium War, the British are destroying Chinese junks which are the ships with unfurled square sails.

THE EARLY YEARS

Confucius, as well as Chinese history. He also read biographies of great figures from other countries, such as U.S. president Abraham Lincoln and British prime minister William Gladstone.

For the next five years, Mao spent his days at school and his spare time helping his father in the fields and keeping the farm records. The relationship between the father and the growing boy was tense. The son thought his father was mean and overly strict. The father thought his son did not show enough respect for parental authority.

This map shows the provinces into which modern China is divided, as well as the towns and villages mentioned in this chapter.

Extreme weather, flooding, and bad harvests often brought famine to China. This well-fed priest appears unmoved by starving peasants.

Between mother and son, however, there was a great bond of love and tenderness.

A FAILED MARRIAGE

When Mao reached 13, his father forced him to leave school so that he could devote himself to working on the family farm. In 1908, when Mao was 14, his parents also decided that he should marry. His wife, chosen for him by his parents, was to be a twenty-year-old girl known only as Miss Luo. The marriage was a disaster from the start. Mao refused to sleep with his new wife, who had moved into his parents' house. Soon afterward, he escaped the whole situation by leaving home to live with a friend.

THE MOVE TO CHANGSHA

After the fiasco of his marriage, Mao began to take charge of his own life. His first move was

The three-year-old boy on the right in this 1909 picture is Emperor Puyi. With him are his father, Prince Chun II, and his brother.

to begin studying again. Initially, he attended local schools in and around Shaoshan, but early in 1911, Mao moved to a secondary school in Changsha, the busy capital of Hunan province. It was there that the intelligent but somewhat unsure teenager first took a serious interest in politics and the plight of the ordinary Chinese people.

By this time, disillusionment with Qing rule had reached new heights. Following the death of Guangxu in 1908, Puyi—a three-year-old boy—had become emperor. Puyi was controlled by adult princes who had neither the intelligence nor the will to introduce the reforms that were the very slim and only hope of saving the dynasty. Foreign interference continued to be a source of collective national humiliation. Other difficulties were stoking up unrest among China's millions of rural peasants. Floods, famines, and the excessive rents demanded by landlords all combined to make life a constant struggle.

THE 1911 REVOLUTION

By late 1911, Mao Zedong was committed to fighting against the empire. He had even cut off his queue, the long braid that the Qing—who were not Chinese but Manchus—forced Chinese men to wear. Mao had also become a follower of Sun Yat-sen, a Chinese nationalist revolutionary who at that time lived in Japan. While living in Japan, Sun led the Revive China Society and taught thousands of visiting Chinese about his ideas.

The spark necessary to ignite revolution was soon struck. On October 9, 1911, in Hankou, central China, a bomb accidentally exploded in the house of a Sun Yat-sen supporter. When Qing officials raided the house, they found evidence of organized anti-imperial activity and responded by executing three of the movement's leaders. Far from crushing the revolutionary movement, the executions led to a major uprising in nearby Wuchang the next day. It quickly spread across the country with unstoppable force.

THE EARLY YEARS

Soon Mao Zedong not only learned of these explosive events, but also felt their effects. On October 22, the city of Changsha was handed over to the revolutionaries and new civil and military governors were installed. Like many other enthusiastic young men, Mao joined the revolutionary army. Meanwhile, Sun Yat-sen returned from Japan, and on January 1, 1912, he was sworn in as President of China in Nanjing. Eleven days later, Puyi abdicated. More than 2,000 years of imperial history had come to an end.

YUAN SHIKAI

Sun's triumph was short-lived. He simply did not have the military muscle or the political experience to bring order to his strife-torn country. So on February 14, 1912, he handed power over to Yuan Shikai, a general who had led the northern armies of the Qing during the dying days of imperial rule. A shrewd operator, Yuan was willing to change sides in return for a high-ranking position in the new republic.

It soon became clear, however, that even Yuan Shikai could not control the forces unleashed in China by the fall of the empire. In any case, he was more interested in building up his own personal power than in smoothing the path to a new, more peaceful China. In 1913, Sun Yat-sen, who had founded the Kuomintang (Nationalist Party) a year earlier, launched an unsuccessful "Second Revolution" against Yuan. After this attempt, Yuan exerted his influence through governors in many provinces, including Hunan. In southern pro-Nationalist areas, however, his rule was weak.

A NEW START FOR MAO

During the spring of 1912, in the midst of this political uncertainty, Mao Zedong left the army. A year later, at age 19, he began a teacher training course at Changsha's Fourth Provincial Normal School. Mao was a diligent student who plunged himself into a wide range of subjects, including Chinese and European philosophy. At the same time, he slowly began to formulate his own ideas about the best way forward for his country.

Japan, meanwhile, continued to exploit China's weakness. In 1915, with all the major European powers preoccupied by World War I (1914–1918), Japan presented Yuan Shikai with its "Twenty-One Demands." These demands amounted to a request to turn China into a Japanese protectorate. Although Yuan stood firm against the more outrageous demands, he gave Japan control of parts of Shandong, the former German sphere of influence, Manchuria, and Inner Mongolia. Mao, like many others, was appalled at this affront to China's national dignity.

Sun Yat-sen (center, to the left of the short man in the dark uniform) with members of the Kuomintang.

The Changsha school where Mao trained as a teacher, and two recent employees. The school burned down in 1938 but was reconstructed.

POLITICAL ACTIVITY

Spurred on by his sense of shame and anger, Mao increased his involvement in political activity. He was particularly inspired by a magazine called *New Youth*, founded in 1915. Its writers called on the young people of China to adopt the economic dynamism, political democracy, and spirit of scientific inquiry found in the West to overthrow the old ways of life and thought that were holding the country back. But although Mao was inspired, he was not overwhelmed. In his view, Chinese philosophers, such as Confucius, also had much to teach China.

The determination of a few young people was not enough to remedy China's problems. In fact, the situation was worsening. Yuan Shikai had proclaimed himself emperor in 1915, only to be met with mass military opposition. This opposition came especially from the south, where in May 1916, a nationalist republic was declared in Guangzhou. A month later, having abandoned his imperial dream, Yuan died. From then on, the Beijing government was unable to control the feuding provincial warlords, and much of China fell into near anarchy.

AN END AND A BEGINNING

Despite all this upheaval, which was felt in Hunan province as elsewhere, Mao continued his training as a teacher. In April 1917, he published an article in *New Youth*. Called "A Study of Physical Education," it stressed the importance of having a strong, fit body. A fit body would, Mao argued, lead to improved understanding, harmonious emotions, and, above all, a strong will. His belief in the importance of a strong will—and in the associated virtues of courage and perseverance—remained throughout his long political career.

Mao had other successes during 1917. In particular, he was elected Student of the Year and became head of the Students' Society. But his student years were soon to end. In June 1918, Mao received his teaching diploma. Uncertain of what to do next, he continued to study privately, and in August, at age 24, he accompanied some friends to Beijing. A new era of his life was about to begin.

Intense but unsure of the way ahead—Mao Zedong in 1919.

IMPERIAL CHINA

Because Mao Zedong's favorite subject was history, he knew a great deal about the emperors who ruled China after it became a united country in 221 B.C. He particularly admired two of these emperors— Qin Shihuangdi and Han Wudi—and sometimes compared himself to them. Of course, when Mao was born in 1893, the empire was not just history. The Qing dynasty lasted until 1911 and the legacy of imperial rule far longer.

On these two pages you can learn a little about how the emperors ruled China, especially during the Qing period. You can also read about the two emperors that Mao Zedong respected most and discover the reasons why.

IMPERIAL RULE

For more than 2,000 years, China was ruled by emperors from a succession of dynasties, or families that ruled for generations. There were eight main dynasties, as well as lesser families who ruled at times when the empire was disunited and rival groups struggled for control.

The emperors had absolute power. They were not only political leaders but also, according to Confucius, "Sons of Heaven." This meant they ruled with divine authority and had to please Heaven by acting correctly and offering prayers and sacrifices. The Chinese believed that if an emperor failed to rule as he should, Heaven would be angry, and disasters and revolts would follow.

KEEPING CONTROL

During the first dynasty, the Qin dynasty (221–207 B.C.), China was divided into provinces, and a strong central administration was set up. By Qing times, there were two main central government offices, the Grand Secretariat and Grand Council. There was also a Punishment Board that ensured obedience to the law. The central government controlled the local governments in the provinces.

The officials who ran the government won their posts by passing examinations about Confucian philosophy and other subjects. By Qing times, however, the government was in a disastrous state. The exams had little to do with ordinary life, and officials were often poor at their jobs. In addition, there were not enough officials—a district magistrate was responsible for up to 250,000 people. Also, many officials were corrupt, keeping some of the taxes they collected. Their corruption was responsible for turning many Chinese against imperial rule.

The Hall of Prayer for Good Harvests in Beijing, where emperors performed religious rituals.

QIN SHIHUANGDI

Qin Shihuangdi was born in 259 B.C., when China was made up of warring states. He ruled a state called Qin, which by 221 B.C. had defeated the other states and united them into one nation. Qin Shihuangdi was its first emperor, beginning the Qin dynasty.

Until his death in 210 B.C., the emperor used his phenomenal energies to shape China according to his wishes. He established a strong central administration in his capital, Xianyang, and built roads linking the city to the provinces. He also introduced single forms of currency and writing and linked various existing walls to form the first Great Wall of China to keep out northern invaders.

Qin Shihuangdi did not allow criticism of his government and banned discussions about politics. He also organized the burning of books on philosophy. Hundreds of scholars who objected to this practice were buried alive.

Many Chinese later criticized Qin Shihuangdi for his ruthless intolerance. But Mao praised it. When people compared him to the "Tiger of Qin," he replied, "You accuse us of acting like Qin Shihuangdi. You are wrong. We surpass him a hundred times. When you berate us for imitating his despotism, we are happy to agree! Your mistake was that you did not say so enough."

Over 7,000 terra-cotta soldiers were buried near Qin Shihuangdi's tomb in Xi'an, north China.

HAN WUDI

Han Wudi was an emperor of the Han dynasty (206 B.C.–A.D. 220). His 54-year reign began in 141 B.C., and he filled it with a whirlwind of activity. He is best remembered, however, for one particular type of activity—war. Han Wudi's armies expanded China to the south and west. They were also successful against the Xiongnu people to the north, whose raids had made a Great Wall necessary. Han Wudi extended the wall for further protection against them.

It was especially for his success in war that Mao Zedong held Han Wudi, also known as the "Martial Emperor," in high esteem. He praised both him and Qin Shihuangdi in his autobiography. However, in one of the many poems that he wrote about China, Mao implied he was their superior:

The Great Wall today.

SNOW

This is the scene in that northern land;
A hundred leagues are sealed with ice,
A thousand leagues of whirling snow.
On either side of the Great Wall
One vastness is all you see . . .
Lured by such great beauty in our landscape
Innumerable heroes have rivaled one another to bow in homage.

But alas, Qin Shihuangdi and Han Wudi
Were rather lacking in culture . . .
To find heroes in the grand manner
We must look rather in the present.

Qin Shihuangdi

CHAPTER TWO

FINDING A ROAD

When Mao arrived in Beijing in 1918, his mind was already teeming with ideas. Chinese philosophy, nationalism, Western political theories, and more were all competing for his allegiance. Once he had reached the capital, where the former child-emperor Puyi was still living in the Forbidden City palace complex, he set out to discover the way forward. The time had come for him to "find a road."

LIBRARIAN MAO

Mao had a trusted friend already living in Beijing: his philosophy teacher from Changsha, Professor Yang Changji. Yang introduced the new arrival to Beijing University librarian Li Dazhao, who offered Mao a job as a library assistant. The position was lowly and the wages meager, so Mao had to live in a cold, crowded courtyard house with seven students. Nevertheless, he relished the chance to learn from the people he met in the intellectual hothouse of the capital.

The man from whom he probably learned most was Li Dazhao himself, who had just become coeditor of *New Youth* magazine. Li was open to the wisdom of both Chinese and Western thought, and he had developed a particular new and burning interest. In the Russian Revolution of 1917, Communists had overthrown the ruling czar. The political philosophy of German thinker Karl Marx had been a major inspiration for their actions, and Li had come to believe that Marxism had much to offer China as well.

Li first made this idea clear in a 1918 *New Youth* article called "The Victory of Bolshevism." He claimed that the Russian Revolution was the cue for "20th-century world revolution" and symbolized "the victory of the spirit of all mankind." In a 1919 newspaper article, Li also stressed the importance of bringing revolution to China's peas-

Beijing early in the 20th century, much as it looked when Mao first arrived there.

ants; "If they are not liberated, then our whole nation will not be liberated," he wrote. Mao read and debated these and many other ideas during his stay in Beijing. But at this stage, neither he nor Li Dazhao considered themselves Marxists. There was much more thinking to be done.

RETURN TO CHANGSHA

Mao Zedong left Beijing in March 1919 to return to Changsha. By the time he reached the city, his mother was seriously ill in a hospital there. She died in October, to Mao's great sorrow. His father outlived her by only a few months.

Gradually, Mao rebuilt his life in Changsha. To earn his living, he worked as a history teacher. But political events soon dominated his existence. In 1917, China entered World War I on the side of the Allies against Germany. The war ended with Germany's defeat in 1918, and a year later, the Paris Peace Conference divided up Germany's former foreign territories among the victors. China had hoped to receive back the once German-controlled, now Japanese-controlled areas in Shandong. The Allies, however, confirmed them as Japanese.

THE MAY FOURTH INCIDENT

This decision, made at the end of April, provoked fury in China. This anger was directed not only at the foreign governments that had disregarded Chinese claims, but also at the Beijing government, which had failed to stand up for Chinese interests. On May 4, 1919, anger turned to violence when a group of about 3,000 students staged a demonstration in Beijing, in which one minister was savagely beaten and many protesters were arrested. Other events in the capital sparked waves of nationalist feeling elsewhere in China, and the country plunged into even greater political turmoil.

In Mao's home province of Hunan,

protests against the Japanese and other foreigners were limited because the local warlord had banned them. Nevertheless, many Hunanese boycotted Japanese goods and displayed anti-Japanese posters. During this time, Mao was thinking about China's underlying problems. He spent many hours considering what was necessary to bring about national renewal. In his view, there could be no half measures. Only the total reform of Chinese society would suffice.

NEW IDEAS

Mao revealed his thinking in a three-part article he wrote in 1919 for a new magazine called the *Xiang River Review*. Its title was "The Great Union of the Popular Masses," and in it, Mao stated that the millions of ordinary Chinese needed to rebel against the aristocrats, capitalists, and others who were oppressing

Chinese people taking part in the May 4, 1919, protests in Beijing.

The Chinese version of the Communist Manifesto appeared in 1920.

them. To back up his case, he cited the examples of the French and Russian Revolutions, in which the masses had rid themselves of power-hungry rulers. The Chinese, he claimed, could do the same. They needed only to organize and believe.

In late 1919 and early 1920, during a second trip to Beijing, Mao's political ideas developed further. By this time, Li Dazhao was more committed to Marxist views, in particular to the idea that radical change in society's economic framework was needed before anything else could follow. The outlook of Li and other friends greatly influenced Mao, as did *The Communist Manifesto* (1847–1848), which had just appeared in Chinese. Written by Karl Marx and Friedrich Engels, it outlined core Communist beliefs.

MARRIAGE AND MARXISM

Mao returned to Changsha in June 1920, where he became head of a primary school. He also got married, this time to a woman he loved. She was Yang Kaihui, the daughter of Professor Yang Changji, and over the next seven years, the couple had three sons. Mao's personal life, however, did not distract him

Mao's second wife, Yang Kaihui, with two of their sons, Anqing and Anying.

Russian Communist leader Vladimir Lenin speaking in Moscow's Red Square in 1919.

from thinking about politics. Still unsure about Marxism when he had left Beijing, by late 1920, he thought of himself as a Marxist.

THE CHINESE COMMUNIST PARTY

Communist Russia, under the leadership of Vladimir Lenin, was by this time taking an interest in China's political upheavals. Early in 1920, it sent representatives to help the Chinese establish Communist study groups. These groups soon sprang up in several cities, and in October, Mao became a founding member of the Changsha cell. By 1921, Russian plans were under way to help China's ardent new Communists to found their own party. The Russians drafted a manifesto and called 13 delegates, Mao among them, to a meeting in Shanghai.

The meeting began on July 23 and lasted for over a week. Arguments raged between delegates about what type of party they wanted. In particular, they found it hard to agree about whether classical Marxism, as applied in Russia, was suitable for China. Sometimes, the Russian representatives intervened to guide the discussions, but they did not always get their way.

In the end, Marxism won the day. The new Chinese Communist Party (CCP) pledged to overthrow China's capitalist class, establish a dictatorship of the proletariat, and work for a classless society. They planned to shun the Beijing government and the Kuomintang, a policy that the Russians believed was a mistake. Nor did China's millions of peasants play a part in the CCP's plan. Instead, the CCP planned to join with the far smaller number of industrial workers, who, in accordance with Marxist theory, were to lead the revolution forward.

At this stage, there were only about 70 CCP members in all of China. But they went back to their homes full of plans. Mao founded the Hunan branch of the CCP in October 1922. He had found his road and was preparing to walk along it.

MARXISM

The political theory devised by the 19th-century German philosopher and economist Karl Marx (below) teaches that human history passes through three phases—first feudalism, then capitalism, and finally communism. According to Marx's theory, the inevitable move from one phase to the next is caused by changing economic conditions. In the capitalist phase, a small proportion of the people owns the factories and other places of work. This group employs industrial workers—known collectively as the proletariat—at low wages and grows rich from the profits of their businesses. In contrast, the wage-earning proletariat grows increasingly poor.

According to Marx, the inevitable result of this situation is that unrest will spread and the proletariat will rise in revolution. After the revolution, the proletariat will lead society, a phenomenon known as the dictatorship of the proletariat. Factories and other property will be owned by all, and a classless communist society ultimately will emerge.

CHINESE PHILOSOPHIES

Three great belief systems held sway in China when Mao Zedong was growing up—Confucianism, Taoism, and Buddhism. Mao studied the first two at school and in his own private reading, while he learned some Buddhist ideas from his mother. Confucianism, in particular, greatly influenced the development of his thought. During the Cultural Revolution, however, Mao publicly turned against every philosophy except his own interpretation of Marxism. Many ideas from Chinese philosophy, nonetheless, run through his Marxist writings.

Here, you can learn a little about Confucianism, Taoism, and Buddhism, and also about the ways in which they influenced Mao.

CONFUCIANISM

Confucius lived in China from 551 to 479 B.C., during a time when the country was divided into many rival states. He was born in the northeastern town of Qufu, but as an adult, he roamed the land teaching different rulers about the philosophy that he had devised.

CONFUCIUS' TEACHINGS

Confucianism is often considered to be a philosophy rather than a religion because it is concerned more with correct thought and action than with the idea of God. Confucius taught that moral behavior and correct relationships were essential if society is to be well-ordered and harmonious. Rulers, for example, had an obligation to please Heaven and to treat their subjects with kindness, while subjects owed their rulers loyalty and obedience. Parents had a duty to care for their children and children a duty to respect their parents. Education was also a vital part of a good society, as it enabled people to distinguish right from wrong.

After Confucius' death, his disciples collected his sayings in a book known as *The Analects*. Knowledge of this work eventually became required for any man who wished to take the examinations for the imperial civil service. As a result, Confucianism became a fundamental part of imperial society.

An artist's impression of Confucius.

MAO AND CONFUCIUS

Mao Zedong had a deep understanding of Confucian thought, which he had studied from an early age. In 1920, he even went to visit Confucius' grave in Qufu. Mao admired the Confucian emphasis on the importance of moral thoughts and actions and on people's making deliberate choices, enforced by their wills, to act in a moral way. He pointed out the need for people to cultivate their own morality by quoting from *The Analects*: "What the superior man seeks is in himself."

In his later years, Mao denounced Confucianism, largely because it praised many of the relationships—emperor and subject, landlord and peasant, even husband and wife—that he came to regard as exploitative. Through Marxism, Mao aimed to free peasants, workers, and others from such bonds. His emphasis, however, on the great importance of education— particularly the study of Chinese history— and on purity of thought and action had its roots in traditional Confucian thought.

TAOISM

No one is sure when Taoism began in China. Laozi, the man said to have founded the philosophy in the 6th century B.C., was almost certainly a legendary figure. The two main Taoist books—the *Tao De Jing* and the *Zhuangzi*—contain a wide variety of ideas. But at their heart is a belief in the Tao, or Way, a mystical force present in everything. Taoists teach that people should live in harmony with this force. To do so, they should aim to bring together opposite aspects of themselves, such as male and female or mind and body, known collectively as Yin and Yang. But they should not try too hard, as this excessive effort would itself make harmony impossible.

Mao sometimes quoted Taoist works in his writings. For example, in his article "A Study of Physical Education," he used these words from the *Zhuangzi*: "A branch in the forest is sufficient for the bird to lodge in, and if it drinks at the river it does not drink more than its stomach can hold." With these words, he was advising readers not to be confused by the many different types of exercise available—one type, regularly practiced, would provide all the benefits needed.

An artist's impression of Laozi.

The Yin (dark) and Yang (light) symbol surrounded by the Eight Trigrams, groups of lines used to foretell the future.

BUDDHISM

Buddhism was founded in India, probably during the 5th century B.C., and had reached China by the first century A.D. The religion's founder, a prince called Gautama Siddhartha, became known as the Buddha, or "enlightened one," after spending a long period in meditation. After this period, he began to teach that the suffering in the world was inevitable, but that through meditation and "right action" and following a series of rebirths, people could escape into the blessed state of nirvana. In this state, the spirit would be freed from the body and suffering would be over. In China, special types of Buddhist belief developed, some of them influenced by Taoism.

Mao knew Chinese forms of Buddhism had played an important part in his country's history, so as a young man, he planned to study them. But after Marxism began to dominate his life, he abandoned this plan.

These are two of the 51,000 carved Buddhist figures dating from about A.D. 5 in the Yungang Caves in Shanxi province.

CHAPTER THREE

COMMUNISTS AND NATIONALISTS

From 1921 to 1927, relations between the Chinese Communist Party (CCP) and the Kuomintang changed, as the two first drew closer together then split dramatically apart. Mao's fortunes also fluctuated, as he rethought his views about how to transform China.

SCHOOLS AND STRIKES

In the early 1920s, Mao left his teaching job and devoted himself to building up the Communist Party in Hunan. He set up a self-study university and a network of night schools where ordinary people could learn about Marxist ideas. He also established trade unions for industrial workers and organized strikes. It was not long before he was called to take a role on the national stage.

THE CCP AND THE KUOMINTANG

The CCP had always refused to work with Sun Yat-sen's Kuomintang. The Soviets (Russia had become the Soviet Union, also known as the Union of Soviet Socialist Republics, or the USSR, in 1922), however, thought that the Nationalists had to play a part in transforming China. They got their way when the 1923 CCP congress accepted that the Communists and the Nationalists should form a united front. It was also declared that Communists should join the Kuomintang, as agreed with Sun Yat-sen, while keeping their own party allegiance.

The 1923 CCP congress was important for Mao because he was elected to the Central Committee. He moved to Shanghai, joined the Kuomintang, and worked closely with its members to forge new policies acceptable to both parties. This was not an easy task, but the Kuomintang slowly became a broader-based party, more open to China's poor peasants and workers.

A TURNING POINT

Despite these events, by late 1924, Mao was depressed because the CCP was scarcely growing, and the warlords were still in power. Eventually, the situation made him ill, so he returned to Changsha, then Shaoshan. This was a turning point for Mao. Deep in China's countryside, he began to organize peasants into associations where they could learn about politics and other subjects. During this time, Mao started to believe that peasants—not industrial workers—were the key to revolution in China. Two more obvious changes also affected China's political landscape in 1925. On March 12, Kuomintang leader Sun Yat-sen died and was soon replaced by General Chiang Kai-shek.

On May 30, British-controlled police in Shanghai fired on demonstrators who were protesting strikebreaking by provincial warlords and foreign influence in China. Four demonstrators were killed and many more injured. The incident fanned the flames of nationalist feeling and was a major spur to Mao's renewed revolutionary zeal among the peasants.

Mao's activities made him no friends among the Hunanese landlords, who did not approve of

Born in 1887, Chiang Kai-shek., like Mao, took part in the revolution that ended imperial rule.

British sailors were called in to help police keep order in Shanghai after the fatal shootings of May 30, 1925.

the peasants' newfound political interests. In the fall of 1925, an order went out to arrest him, and Mao was forced to flee. He made his way to Guangzhou, where the Kuomintang had established a government. There, he became leader of the party's Propaganda Department, edited a political newspaper, and ran classes for peasants at the Peasant Movement Training Institute.

THE NORTHERN EXPEDITION

Sun Yat-sen had planned to organize a military expedition starting from his southern base that would defeat the warlords as he advanced north and unite the country. In 1926, Chiang Kai-shek set out to make Sun's dream a reality, but the Soviets who were in China to advise the Kuomintang put obstacles in his way. Chiang already considered the Communists to be too influential in his party, so on March 20, he arrested both the Soviets and all the local Chinese Communists.

The incident was quickly over, and the Soviets ended their objections to the so-called Northern Expedition. But following the Communists' release, the Nationalists'

ruling committee removed many CCP members from high-ranking posts within the Kuomintang. Mao lost his position as head of the Propaganda Department, but he was allowed to continue teaching peasants. Finally, in July, Chiang led his troops north on their mission to unite the country.

POWER TO THE PEASANTS

Mao, meanwhile, devoted himself to educating peasants in the south. But with the approval of the Nationalists and the Soviets, he also sent trainees into areas the Northern Expedition was to invade. Once there, they explained their ideas to the peasants, hoping that these people would then welcome Chiang's armies. The trainees also stayed after the armies had gone to consolidate support and stir up revolts against local landlords.

The CCP, which as a whole had been slow to accept the importance of the peasants in preparing for revolution, now realized its mistake. As a result, it set up its Peasant Department, with Mao as its leader. He left Guangzhou to take up his new role in Shanghai in November 1926. In December, he went to Changsha for the First Congress of the Hunan Provincial Peasants' Association. Following that, in early 1927, Mao went on a fact-finding mission through the Hunan

21

THE NORTHERN EXPEDITION

During the summer of 1926, Kuomintang troops set out on the Northern Expedition from their strongholds in the southern provinces of Guangdong and Guangxi. While some took a central route, seizing Changsha on August 21, others made their way up the coast. Shanghai fell on March 22, 1927, and Nanjing, which became the Nationalist capital, fell two days later. The Kuomintang did not, however, manage to take Beijing until 1928.

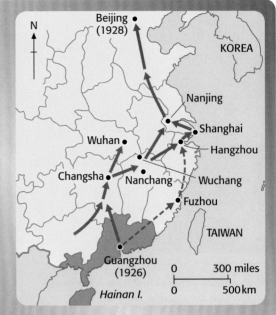

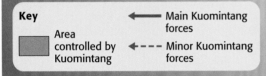

Key
- Area controlled by Kuomintang
- ⟵ Main Kuomintang forces
- ⟵--- Minor Kuomintang forces

countryside. What he saw altered his thinking radically and permanently.

REVOLUTIONARY REPORT

Mao recounted his findings in his "Report of an Investigation into the Peasant Movement in Hunan." It made clear that, far from being unprepared for revolution, as Mao had believed, the peasants were impressively well organized. In fact, by late 1926, they had already risen up against many landlords.

The conclusion Mao drew from his new knowledge, in the report's words, was that, "In a very short time, several hundred million peasants...will rise like a tornado or tempest. . . ." The CCP, however, was unsure this was the best approach to support. Many of its members were still unconvinced that peasants should be the driving force for change. Nor did they want further to alienate the Kuomintang, which was wary of the upheaval already sweeping parts of rural China.

THE END OF UNITY

In any event, their cautiousness came too late. Chiang Kai-shek was growing more and

more concerned that the left wing of the Kuomintang was moving closer to the Communists and turning against his leadership. Chiang, therefore, decided to strike first. In March 1927, his armies seized Shanghai. Then, in the early hours of April 12, they launched a vicious attack on the Communists in the city. At least 400 were killed. The united front, always an uneasy alliance, had received a severe blow.

The Communists did not know how to respond. Should they break entirely with the Kuomintang or should they try to make a deal with its left wing? And should they reduce their efforts to stir up unrest in the countryside? Mao, now running the All China Peasants' Association and planning the redistribution of landlords' fields to the poor, was deeply opposed to this last idea. It soon became clear that there was no way back.

While the Communist leaders argued among themselves, the Nationalists continued their attacks on ordinary CCP members in many areas. Finally, on May 21, 1927, a major anti-Communist uprising took place in and around Changsha. It was led by the city's military commander and local Kuomintang forces that opposed the activities of the peasant associations. By the time the savagery was over, hundreds of thousands of people were dead. Similar crackdowns on Communists began in other provinces.

THE AUTUMN HARVEST UPRISING

By late in the summer of 1927, the CCP was in disarray. Its alliance with the Kuomintang was effectively over, it had no serious military strength, and the peasant movement in Hunan had been all but crushed. But in August, a backlash against Nationalist repression began, and a Communist uprising occurred in Nanchang, the capital of Jiangxi. Meanwhile, Mao and other CCP members were in Hankou to plan a similar uprising in Hunan. Mao was made Special Commissioner for the province, and on August 12, he left for Changsha. On September 9, a force of workers, peasants, and ex-Kuomintang troops launched their attack on the Kuomintang forces.

The Hunan rebellion, known as the Autumn Harvest Uprising, ended in disaster. The 3,000-strong Communist force was not large or skillful enough to defeat the Kuomintang troops. Mao led the remaining Communist forces east into the Jinggang Mountains on the Jiangxi province border. They settled there in October and were gradually joined by refugee forces from failed revolts in Nanchang and elsewhere.

Chinese peasants gleefully burn the deeds that proclaimed their landlords' ownership of the land they struggled to work.

CHAPTER FOUR

WAR AND REVOLUTION

The Communists' seven-year retreat to Jiangxi and other mountain areas of China was not a retreat from their struggle. Conflict with the Nationalists, who were now based in the new capital of Nanjing, continued with equal fervor after the disasters of 1927. In 1949, after more than 20 years of war and revolution, the Communists emerged victorious. So, too, did Mao Zedong.

MOUNTAIN MEN

In late 1927, Mao's position was not promising. He was stranded in the Jinggang Mountains with a few poorly armed troops, peasants, and workers, and he had fallen from favor with the CCP because of the failure of the Autumn Harvest Uprising. But Mao recovered quickly and established a Communist-style government among both his men and the local peasant communities. His position improved in April 1928, when Zhu De, future commander of the Red Army, arrived from Nanchang. The two men's troops united to create a force of about 8,000.

LOVE AND WAR

Over the following months, Mao learned military skills—including guerrilla warfare techniques—to add to his already well-developed abilities as a political operator. Kuomintang forces repeatedly attacked the Communists through the bamboo-covered slopes of the mountains, and Mao and Zhu De repeatedly drove them back. At the same time, discipline, training, and commitment were turning the two leaders' once ramshackle troops into a serious fighting force, the beginnings of the mighty Red Army.

There were also developments in Mao's personal life. In summer 1928, he met an 18-year-old girl named He Zizhen and made her his third wife. His second wife, Yang Kaihui, was still in Changsha and was heartbroken when she heard the news. In 1930, after the Communist attack on Changsha, Yang Kaihui was executed by the Nationalists.

CONFLICTING VIEWS

A difference of opinion emerged among Communists about how to continue the fight against the Kuomintang. In an October 1928 report called "Why is it that Red [Communist] Political Power Exists in China?," Mao outlined his view. Communist government and land reform, he said, should first be introduced in small "base areas," such as his own base in Jiangxi. Guerrilla warfare should then be waged from there. In this way, the strength of the CCP, the peasants, and the emerging Red Army could develop gradually. Only then could the Communists fight the Kuomintang nationally with any real hope of success.

The main opponent of Mao's theory was Li Lisan, then head of the CCP. He still believed that Communists should begin uprisings in the cities, stir the proletariat up to revolution, and then allow them to lead nationwide conflict. In June 1930, the CCP Politburo adopted Li Lisan's "line," or policy, and Communist forces, including the army led by Mao and Zhu De, were ordered to prepare for city attacks in July. But after early gains by the Communists, particularly in Changsha, the Nationalists forced them back into the mountains, and Li Lisan was dismissed.

ENCIRCLEMENT CAMPAIGNS

Shortly after this setback for the Communists, Chiang Kai-shek stepped up his attacks against the Red Army in Jiangxi province. In the first "encirclement and suppression campaign," launched in December 1930, Chiang marched 100,000 troops against his enemy. But by this time, the Communists were a disciplined force of about 40,000 men, including local peasants. Using a new strategy in which, by withdrawing, they forced the Nationalists to advance deep into enemy territory and then attacked them, Mao's army beat back their opponents in January 1931.

In the spring, the Nationalists started another encirclement campaign, this time with 200,000 men, but the result was the same. A third campaign, begun in July, was well under way when outside events intervened. On September 18, as part of an expansion program designed to gain for themselves more territory and more raw materials for industry, the Japanese invaded the northeastern region known as Manchuria. As a result, Chiang Kai-shek had to turn his attention there and temporarily halt his attacks against the Communists far to the south in Jiangxi.

THE CHINESE SOVIET REPUBLIC

Another important development occurred in the late summer of 1931. The CCP Central

Despite their superior manpower and equipment, Nationalist troops like these were often outmaneuvered by Mao's men.

Committee, which had been operating secretly in Shanghai, now moved to Mao Zedong's base in Jiangxi. Its members, including Mao's future close colleague Zhou Enlai, still believed that the cities and the proletariat should lead the revolution. In their new home, they hoped to curb Mao's attempts to give peasants the major role.

Back in August 1929, Mao and Zhu De had set up a provincial Communist government in the Jiangxi town of Ruijin. On November 7, 1931, the anniversary of the Russian Revolution, the Central Committee proclaimed the founding of the Chinese Soviet Republic. Mao was appointed chairman of this Communist state within a state, which contained about 3 million people. It was not as grand of a position as it sounded; much of the real power in the new republic had been taken over by newcomers from Shanghai.

TWIN ENEMIES

The Communists confronted two enemies in 1932. In April, the Chinese Soviet Republic declared war on the Japanese in Manchuria.

Its priority, however, remained the defeat of the Kuomintang and the establishment of a Communist government across all of China. The Central Committee planned to achieve this by adopting an "offensive line"—that is, by sending troops into Nationalist-controlled cities and other areas. Mao believed the Red Army was not ready for this approach, but his views were dismissed.

Mao's assessment of the military situation proved largely correct. Many Communist attacks on cities failed. Chiang Kai-shek's fourth encirclement campaign, which lasted from April to October 1933, however, was still defeated using Mao-style guerrilla tactics.

Chiang's fifth encirclement campaign, which followed immediately, proved tougher to overcome. Chiang Kai-shek now had 400,000 troops at his disposal, as well as expert German military advisers. Eventually, it became clear that the Nationalists could not be pushed back. The Jiangxi base area would have to be abandoned.

THE LONG MARCH

What followed was a trek of nearly 8,100 miles (13,000 kilometers) to China's northwest that became known as the Long March. About 100,000 Communists left Jiangxi in mid-October 1934. They included Mao's wife, He Zizhen, but their son, Xiao Mao, was left behind and never seen again. The marchers struggled through terrains ranging from arid deserts to snowcapped mountains. Long battles against the Nationalists made their passage still harder to endure. Fewer than 5,000 people survived to reach Wuqi, in Shaanxi province, in October 1935.

During this ordeal, Mao Zedong's political fortunes were transformed. At a meeting held at Zunyi in January 1935, Zhou Enlai and other members of the CCP Politburo acknowledged the serious errors of military judgment they had made in Jiangxi province. They also accepted that Mao's policies had

Mao on horseback in northwest China, as he nears the end of the Long March.

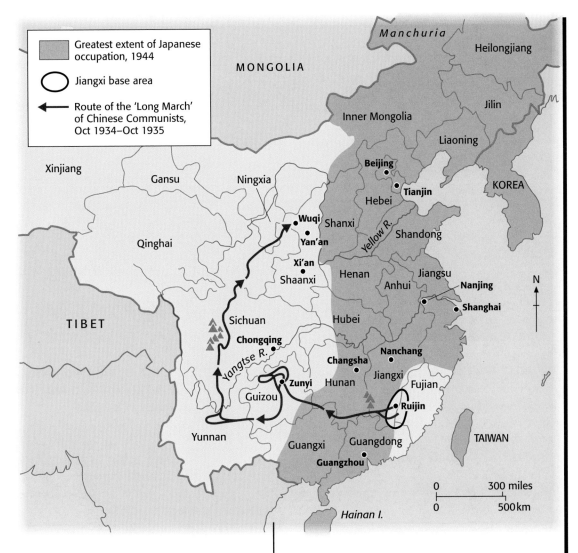

Key:

Greatest extent of Japanese occupation, 1944

Jiangxi base area

Route of the 'Long March' of Chinese Communists, Oct 1934–Oct 1935

This map shows the perilous, winding route of the Long March, which began on October 18, 1934, and ended one year and four days later.

been correct. Mao was made Zhou's chief military adviser, and he led the Long March to its end. Mao was now in control of China's Communists.

REUNITED?

Japan had not been idle in China since its invasion of Manchuria. In 1933, it had made the region into a puppet state called Manchukuo and advanced south. Far from resisting, Chiang Kai-shek had appeased the

invaders. By 1935, when Japan tried to take still more land, the Chinese were demanding a far stronger response. But Chiang refused all Communist offers to form a new united front against the common enemy.

Matters came to a head in December 1936, when Chiang visited a military base in Xi'an. There he urged Nationalists to make one final, decisive encirclement of the Communists. But the men had no wish to fight fellow-Chinese when the Japanese enemy was nearby, so on December 12, they arrested Chiang. When he was released two weeks later, a revival of the idea of a united front seemed at hand. Mao was not so sure.

WORLD WAR II

Mao's caution proved correct. Chiang Kai-shek resisted forming an alliance for months afterwards. But then events forced his hand. On July 7, 1937, Japan launched an attack on the Marco Polo Bridge railway junction, just outside Beijing. This attack began World War II in the Pacific region. By September, Chiang Kai-shek allowed the Nationalists to join the Communists in a combined effort to save China.

Japan's troops proved too strong for even the united Chinese force to resist. From mid-1937, they swept down the east coast of China, capturing large areas of land, including all the major ports and industrial areas. There were not, however, enough Japanese to take over the whole country, so the Nationalist government moved inland to Chongqing. The Communists, meanwhile, remained in Shaanxi and used guerrilla techniques to lead resistance inside Japanese-occupied areas.

NEW IDEAS—AND A NEW WIFE

International events had not distracted Mao from his plans to build a Communist China.

The town of Yan'an, where the Communists settled after the Long March. The tiered building in the center is a pagoda.

The Communists moved from base to base in Shaanxi, finally settling in Yan'an. At each base, they set up a military training institute where Mao gave lectures. Some of these lectures were then published as "Problems of Strategy in China's Revolutionary War" (1936), "On Practice" (1937), and "On Contradiction" (1937). In these three important works, Mao used both Marxist doctrine and Chinese philosophy to outline his ideas about how Marxism should be adapted for China.

In the midst of all his political concerns, Mao did not neglect his personal life. In 1938, he married his fourth and last wife Jiang Qing, a 23-year-old actress from Shanghai. He Zizhen had already left.

ONE WAR ENDS . . .

World War II ended in August 1945, after the United States, by now China's ally, dropped atomic bombs on Japan. The united front between the Communists and the

EDGAR SNOW

Edgar Snow was born in Kansas City, Missouri, in 1905. He began a career in advertising, but then decided to see the world instead. After traveling to Japan as a stowaway, he went to China, where he stayed from 1928 to 1941. In those years, he interviewed several leaders of the Chinese Communist Party. Among them was Mao Zedong, whom Snow visited in Shaanxi province in 1936. Snow's book *Red Star Over China* (1938) is a classic account of Mao and the CCP. The picture below was taken in 1970, when Snow met Mao again, this time in Beijing.

Nationalists had barely survived the war years. Now they again had to decide how to relate to one another in peacetime.

Chiang Kai-shek's inclination was to turn against the CCP. But he knew that the Communists had won great support among the peasants by helping to drive the Japanese from their land. In addition, Communists controlled about two-thirds of the former Japanese-occupied territories, which they called "liberated areas," and had a force of two million soldiers at their command. In contrast, the Nationalists, although they had a five-million-strong army, had already lost considerable support nationwide. Corruption and economic collapse were making them less and less popular.

For his part, Mao Zedong was ready to form a coalition government with the Nationalists if the conditions were right. In August 1945, Mao flew to Chongqing for negotiations with Chiang Kai-shek. By October 10, the two men had come to a general decision to avoid civil war, but there was an ominous lack of agreement over details.

. . . AND ANOTHER BEGINS

Civil war broke out just a month later, in Manchuria. An American mediator, General George C. Marshall, arranged a ceasefire in January 1946, but by June, there was no holding back the two sides. The brutal conflict between the Communists and the Nationalists, temporarily interrupted by World War II, was entering its final phase.

The Nationalists made early gains, especially in the Communist strongholds of northern China. But in 1948, Communist forces, now known as the People's Liberation Army (PLA), struck back. In January 1949, they seized the cities of Tianjin and Beijing; in May, they took Shanghai; and in October, Guangzhou. The result was clear. Nationalist rule was over. Communism had triumphed.

Mao addresses his soldiers in 1944.

CHAPTER FIVE

THE PEOPLE'S REPUBLIC

On October 1, 1949, in the magnificent setting of Tiananmen Square, in Beijing, Mao Zedong proclaimed the founding of the People's Republic of China. Now he would put into practice the Communist ideals that he had refined during long years of struggle. Now he would promise China's 500 million people a future that was "infinitely bright."

PLANNING THE FUTURE

Back in June, Mao had already outlined his plans for the country in a wide-ranging speech called "On the People's Democratic Dictatorship." In particular, he had emphasized the need to give power and land to ordinary people, especially workers and peasants, and to remove it from the control of rich landlords and officials. He had also stressed the importance of building up industry and of educating the rural poor.

A government had been established in Beijing, which had been made China's capital again. Mao was head of state as well as chairman of the CCP, and Zhou Enlai was prime minister. In November 1949, the Nationalist government's departure for the island of Taiwan closed the door on the country's past. Not long after, Mao's December trip to Moscow to meet Soviet leader Joseph Stalin was a sign for the future.

HATRED AND BRUTALITY

As the 1950s opened, the PLA brought the remaining Nationalist strongholds in mainland China and Hainan Island under Communist control. Meanwhile, the government began its campaign against counter-revolutionaries, or opponents of its regime. The campaign was a free-for-all, as supporters of Communism roamed the land beating and killing foreigners, former Nationalists, and others. Mao Zedong fully supported this outpouring of brutality.

The passing of the Agrarian Reform Law on June 30, 1950, also stirred unrest. This law made rules for the confiscation of large estates and the redistribution of land among the poor. But in the troubled atmosphere, peasants began publicly humiliating and executing the landlords who used to own these properties. As many as two million landlords were put to death by mobs in acts of great hysteria and hatred. Another of the early

Mao declared the founding of the People's Republic of China in October 1949.

Many Chinese landlords met this grim fate during the early years of Communist rule.

laws passed under Mao's rule was the 1950 Marriage Law, an attempt to transform marriage customs in China.

CHINA AND THE WORLD

While overseeing massive upheaval at home, the Chinese government also concerned itself with the outside world. On February 14, 1950, China cemented its relationship with the Soviet Union by signing the Treaty of Friendship, Alliance, and Mutual Assistance. In June, the country was plunged unexpectedly into a major foreign-policy crisis.

In that month, the troops of Soviet-backed, Communist North Korea invaded U.S.-backed, non-Communist South Korea. The United States sent in troops, and the Korean War began. Soon, U.S. soldiers advanced across the border from South Korea, and the United Nations also intervened on the side of South Korea. China did not want a U.S.-backed government in North Korea, which lay along its own southeastern border, so in October 1950, Mao sent in troops.

This cartoon shows the Chinese and Koreans combining to chase from Korea, first, the Japanese (above) and, later, U.S. soldiers.

The fighting dragged on until 1953, when an armistice was finally signed. Many thousands of people lost their lives in the indecisive struggle, which left the border between the two countries exactly where it had been at the outset. Among the dead was Mao's oldest son, Anying. When Mao heard the news, he was struck dumb with anguish.

THE THREE AND FIVE ANTIS

In late 1951, Mao's government launched several new campaigns. These included the Three Antis—against corruption, waste, and excessive bureaucracy—and the Five Antis—against both financial crimes and the revealing of state secrets to foreigners. The targets of these campaigns were urban businesspeople. Soon they were suffering abuse and lynchings, as landlords had before them.

THE FIVE-YEAR PLAN

In 1953, as the civil war was receding slowly into memory, the Communist regime launched the Five-Year Plan to modernize Chinese agriculture and industry. This was an idea bor-

THE OCCUPATION OF TIBET

When the Communists came to power in China, the bordering country of Tibet was an independent state. Tibet had been under Chinese rule until 1912, and in 1951, the People's Liberation Army set out to reconquer it. The Tibetans were almost powerless to resist, and their leader, a Buddhist monk known as the Dalai Lama, temporarily fled the country. After a Tibetan uprising in 1959 was suppressed by Chinese troops (below), the Dalai Lama left for good, and he now leads resistance to Chinese rule from India. In 1965, Tibet was made an autonomous region of China, which it unwillingly remains.

rowed from the Soviet Union, where Stalin had begun such long-term planning in 1928. To help China, Stalin sent technical experts to the country. By 1960, more than 1,400 Soviet experts were at work in China.

COLLECTIVE AGRICULTURE

A main aim of the Five-Year Plan was to introduce collective agriculture. The first step was to establish Mutual Aid Teams, or groups of villagers who shared tools and animals, and who worked the land together. Next came Primary Stage Cooperatives, whose members owned some land and tools jointly. They were paid according to how much of their prop-

erty they handed over to collective ownership, and how much work they did. Finally, Advanced Stage Cooperatives were formed. These involved all members of a village jointly owning all land, tools, and animals and receiving payment based only on work done.

The collectivization program did not run smoothly. When villages formed cooperatives without proper planning, they often ended up facing both food shortages and serious debt. In addition, some people simply did not want to share. Many peasants killed their farm animals rather than share them. These problems were worsened by natural disasters, especially the floods that swept across the Yangtse River valley in 1954.

The program also caused disputes among the CCP leadership. Mao wanted to push ahead fast, but other members, particularly Finance Minister Bo Yibo, advised a gradual pace. The result was a yo-yo effect. First, collectivization was driven rapidly forward, then it was cut back just as rapidly. But after Mao made a tour of farms to assess the situation for himself in April 1955, he would accept no compromises. Collectivization was to proceed as quickly as possible. By the end of 1956, 97 percent of the peasant population worked on collective farms.

INDUSTRY AND BUSINESS

The development of industry was another target of the Five-Year Plan. As China had little experience in promoting industrial growth—the emperors had made sure of that—the country had to rely at first on expert help sent from the Soviet Union. The Soviet Union also provided money to set up about 140 huge industrial plants in China, as well as industrial training for thousands of Chinese students in the Soviet Union.

China's industrial planning soon brought huge rises in productivity. For example, the output of steel in 1957 was 6 million tons (5.4 million tonnes), compared with just 174,000 tons (158,000 tonnes) in 1949.

Mao was always eager to increase agricultural production. In this 1958 picture, he encourages a peasant working the soil.

Massive engineering projects were also successfully completed, including a 22,000-foot- (6,700-meter) long bridge across the Yangtse and a major railroad-building program. By 1957, 27,300 miles (44,000 km) of tracks criss-crossed the country, compared with fewer than half that number in 1949.

Mao was eager to ensure that the growth of industry and business in China was achieved in accordance with Communist principles, not just by experts interested only in technical success. He was also determined that business and industry, like agriculture, should be brought under state control. Accordingly, on December 6, 1955, he pro-

claimed that allprivate companies should be in state hands within two years. Business owners anxious not to provoke violent public outbursts against them soon complied.

THE HUNDRED FLOWERS CAMPAIGN

Another important development slowly began in 1956. On May 26, the slogan "Let a hundred flowers blossom, let a hundred schools of thought contend!" was first proclaimed by the CCP, with Mao's full approval. The aim of the following campaign was to encourage intellectuals and others to voice any criticisms that they might have of the government. This was an unexpected step for Mao to take because previously he had been concerned to quash all dissent.

One reason for the change arose from the situation in the Soviet Union, where Nikita Khrushchev had become leader after Stalin's death in 1953. In early 1956, Khrushchev had strongly criticized his predecessor, earning the contempt of Mao, who believed Stalin had been essentially a good Marxist. Mao also looked on with scorn in 1956, as both Poland and Hungary rose up against Soviet rule, only to be crushed. He believed the Soviet government had lost its way, no longer expressing the will of the people but imposing its will on the people. China was not to follow that road— the CCP would listen to the people's wishes.

Another reason for the new campaign was the desire to placate intellectuals, as well as skilled workers and scientists. China needed them to help turn the country into the industrial powerhouse of which Mao dreamed. But under Communist rule, they had faced abuse and repression. Now Mao proclaimed, their views were welcome, and the CCP would no longer exert strict control over their work.

CRITICISM AND REPRESSION

The "Hundred Flowers" Campaign took off in earnest after February 1957, when Mao made a major speech called "On the Correct Handling of Contradictions Among the

Sparks fly as Chinese citizens with no industrial training make doomed attempts to manufacture steel in "backyard furnaces."

People." In it, he proclaimed that differences of opinion, or "contradictions," were inevitable in the early stages of building a Communist society and that it was right to air them. But over the following months, he was horrified to see the extent of the criticism he had unleashed. Students at Beijing University even stuck huge antigovernment posters up on a special "Democracy Wall."

This outspokenness was too much for Mao, so in June, he struck back with the Anti-Rightist Campaign. The true purpose of the Hundred Flowers Campaign, he declared, had been to draw rightists, or opponents of communism, out into the open so they could be punished. Over half a million intellectuals were sent to labor camps or shipped to the countryside to learn Communist ideals from the peasant masses.

THE GREAT LEAP FORWARD

In May 1958, Mao launched headlong into a new venture. This was China's second Five-Year Plan, which became known as the Great Leap Forward. The scheme was overly ambitious. Agricultural and industrial production were to soar—for example, 110 million tons

(100 million tonnes) of steel were to be produced in 1962, 20 times the prior annual amount. Coal and electricity outputs were also to reach new heights. But Mao's aims were not purely economic. Commitment to Communism was also to leap forward.

To bring about this dynamic growth, the population of the Chinese countryside was reorganized into huge communes, each containing up to 40,000 people, or about 6,000 families. The CCP tried deliberately to break down family ties by encouraging everyone to eat in communal mess halls and to sleep in large single-sex dormitories. Children were to be raised in public nurseries, while the elderly were to spend their final days in "Happiness Homes."

Working life on the new communes was harsh. Divided into groups called brigades, people were expected to labor late into the night to achieve the unrealistic productivity goals set by the CCP. The brigades had neither the expertise nor the equipment to carry out the tasks demanded of them. To make steel, many built inefficient "backyard furnaces." Having no wood to fuel their furnaces, they cut down fruit trees, and having no iron, they melted down cooking pots to produce the necessary raw material. The results of all this sacrifice were minimal. Most of the steel they produced was of such poor quality it was unusable.

The Great Leap Forward also failed in another way. The millions of peasants devoting themselves to industrial work could not also tend crops in the fields, so food production did not rise as fast as Mao had predicted. Food shortages were made worse by floods. Between 1959 and 1960, about 20 million Chinese people starved to death.

The failure of the Great Leap Forward led to guarded criticism of Mao by other prominent members of the CCP. Probably as a result of this criticism, Mao announced in December 1958 that he was giving up his role as head of state. Liu Shaoqi took over in April 1959. Mao, however, remained in place as Chairman of the Party. In 1960, the Great Leap Forward finally was abandoned.

SPLITTING WITH THE SOVIETS

Tensions between Mao and Soviet leader Nikita Khrushchev had grown during the 1950s. Mao deplored the Soviet Union's attempts to dictate China's atomic weapons policy as well as its efforts towards peace with the United States, the enemy of Communism. Khrushchev could not understand Mao's unwillingness to cooperate with his plans and was appalled by the communes' excesses.

Finally, in 1960, the enmity between the two Communist powers came out into the open. The Soviet Union withdrew its technicians from China in April and soon ended all financial aid. Still reeling from the Great Leap Forward, the Chinese stood alone. But Mao, convinced he was now the true leader of world Communism, was undaunted.

Mao and Soviet leader Nikita Khrushchev in the friendly times before the bitter 1960 split between their two countries.

CHAPTER SIX

THE CULTURAL REVOLUTION AND AFTER

In the early 1960s, new head of state Liu Shaoqi and General Secretary of the CCP Deng Xiaoping led China's recovery. Many communes were broken up, and private ownership of land and businesses was once again permitted. At first, Mao had little choice but to accept this assault on the purity of his Marxist ideals, but eventually, he could take it no more and again set out to restore power to the masses—whatever the cost.

DIFFERING VIEWS

Deng Xiaoping liked to sum up his approach to politics by quoting an ancient Chinese proverb: "What does it matter if the cat is black or white as long as it catches mice?" In other words, if a policy has the desired effect, its precise details are not especially important. For Mao, however, adherence to strict Marxist doctrine was essential. He made his views clear at a CCP meeting in September 1962, where he urged delegates to remember the class struggle and to oppose revisionism—that is, the belief that Marxism should evolve away from a revolutionary ideal.

THE SOCIALIST EDUCATION MOVEMENT

Mao's status in the CCP was so high that Liu and Deng, although technically in charge of the country, often gave way to his demands. In the aftermath of the 1962 meeting, they launched the Socialist Education Movement. It organized meetings in both urban and rural areas, where the virtues of Communism were praised and the vices of capitalism denounced. The movement also worked to root out revisionism and corruption, especially among local party cadres, or groups of officials. As so often in the past, excessive zeal led to widespread violence and executions.

Mao was still not content with the diluted form of Communism that he believed the CCP was following. In his view, nothing less than a revival of revolution would stop China from sliding back into its old ways. The problem was that Liu Shaoqi and Deng Xiaoping, whom Mao now thought of as "capitalist roaders," or followers of capitalism, would never adopt this approach. He, Mao Zedong, would have to act.

BUILDING A BASE

As the CCP was no longer fully under his control, Mao realized he needed to establish a separate power base if he were to have any chance of success. He began to build a close relationship with Lin Biao, Defense Minister

With a poster of Mao behind them, workers prepare to distribute copies of *The Little Red Book of Quotations from Mao Zedong*.

and leader of the People's Liberation Army. Lin soon became Mao's greatest supporter. The defense minister launched Mao's "cult of personality," encouraging worship of Mao as though he were an emperor.

Of particular importance in spreading the Mao cult was a book prepared at Lin Biao's request. *The Little Red Book of Quotations from Mao Zedong* was published in 1964. At first intended only for PLA soldiers, as the decade continued, it became required reading for all Chinese people who considered themselves true followers of Mao.

THE CULTURAL REVOLUTION

Mao planned to begin his new movement by attacking China's arts and educational sys-

In 1966, Mao took a public swim in the Yangtse to show that he was fit and ready for the struggle ahead.

tem. In his judgment, these aspects of Chinese culture had not changed in line with Marxist ideals and were in need of reform. To take the first step, he enlisted the help of his wife, the actress Jiang Qing. The couple were no longer close, but they shared a commitment to radical action.

Mao's Cultural Revolution began in November 1965, with the publication of an article in a Shanghai newspaper. The article criticized a new play whose author was a friend of Peng Zhen, the mayor of Beijing and a top CCP member. Next, in early 1966, Lin Biao invited Jiang Qing to set up a cultural discussion group in the PLA. The group condemned capitalist influence in the arts, promoting "Mao Thought" instead. Both events were veiled attacks on the CCP leadership and its revisionism.

Forced onto the defensive, the Party's Central Committee was unsure how to respond. Finally, on May 16, it issued a circular that declared the CCP should "hold high the great banner of the proletarian cultural revolution." Revisionism in the arts and among Communist Party members was to be ruthlessly rejected. Peng Zhen had already become the first casualty of this new policy. The playwright was purged from the Communist Party before the circular had even been made public.

THE RED GUARDS

Mao had no intention of allowing Liu Shaoqi and other "capitalist roaders" to drive the Cultural Revolution forward. Instead, he established his own headquarters and planned to use the army and political allies such as his wife to spread his ideas. A new group was also emerging that was to play a leading role in the events unfolding across China.

Thanks to Lin Biao's propaganda, the Mao personality cult was growing fast, and students were among its most ardent members. In late May, a group from Qinghua University Middle School in Beijing declared themselves to be "Red Guards," who were devoted to Maoist ideals. Soon students from many other secondary schools and universities were following the same revolutionary path, proclaiming, "We are the critics of the old world; we are the builders of the new."

Mao was delighted by the passion of these young people, and from August to November 1966, he held a series of huge rallies for them in Beijing's Tiananmen Square. There, the students waved their *Little Red Books* and listened to adoring speeches in praise of Mao. Then, in a fever, they went out across the country to do his will.

A Red Guard rally in Beijing during the Cultural Revolution. Young supporters of Mao filled the great Tiananmen Square.

VIOLENCE AND DESTRUCTION

The Red Guards' first targets were their own teachers. The lucky ones were simply forced to wear dunce caps and receive abuse for their revisionist teachings. The unlucky were tied up, then beaten senseless or killed. Red Guard violence was soon also turned against scientists, police officers, and foreigners, as well as against priests and their sacred buildings.

Red Guards did not always stay in their home areas. Traveling around China, they often clashed violently with local Party officials that they thought were "capitalist roaders." Many young people also traveled to Beijing to see Mao for themselves.

PARTY PURGES

In August 1966, at Mao's request, the CCP Central Committee approved the 16-Point Plan for the Cultural Revolution. But in the very same month, Mao also prepared a poster calling on Red Guards to "Bombard the Headquarters," that is, turn against the CCP leadership. Many Party members were soon expelled, but Liu Shaoqi and Deng Xiaoping remained in power until 1968, when they were finally purged.

The expulsion of the two leaders came at a time when Mao was trying to draw the Cultural Revolution to a close. The violence and chaos caused by the Red Guard eventually shocked even him, so in late 1967, he sent in the PLA to restore order. Its soldiers took more than a year to rescue China from the mire into which it had sunk.

LIN BIAO

The years between the end of the Cultural Revolution and Mao's death in 1976 continued to be marked by political dissent. Strict Marxists, including Mao and his wife Jiang Qing, continued to oppose those with a more practical approach, such as Zhou Enlai. In fact, some experts think this era was just another— although less violent—stage of the Cultural Revolution itself.

The next CCP member to fall from favor was Lin Biao, one of Mao's most dutiful supporters during the Cultural Revolution. Mao had made Lin his official successor in 1969, but from then on, the relationship between the two men had deteriorated. This was partly because Mao had come to believe Lin was trying to seize too much power too soon. The Party Chairman also thought that the PLA, which was under Lin Biao's command, was growing far too influential.

Aware of Mao's displeasure, Lin feared he would be purged from the CCP and grew depressed. At the same time, Lin's son, an air-force officer, began to plan first a coup, then the assassination of Mao. When Lin Biao learned of these schemes is unclear, but by the fall of 1971, he certainly knew about them and had found out that Mao also knew. Lin fled China for the Soviet Union on September 12. He was killed when his airplane crashed in Mongolia early the next day. Whether this was an accident or the result of a plot organized by Mao remains uncertain.

MAO AND NIXON

By this time an old man of 77, Mao was deeply distressed by the loss of a once faithful ally. His health suffered as a result, and he visibly began to weaken. For the daily running of the government, he now depended on Prime Minister Zhou Enlai, who did not share Mao's extreme Marxist views but had been wily enough to survive the purges.

At this late stage in his career, urged on by Zhou Enlai, Mao agreed to a major change in

Mao shakes the hand of U.S. president Richard Nixon in 1972. Both set aside their ideological differences for political reasons.

his country's foreign policy. Relations between the Soviet Union and China had grown steadily worse since the split of 1960. The United States remained an enemy, as well, continuing to support the Nationalists in Taiwan and opposing Communist forces both in Korea and during the long-running Vietnam War. In the late 1960s, the situation began to change.

Further deterioration in China's relationship with the Soviet Union was the spur. Mao was appalled when the Soviets invaded Czechoslovakia in 1968 to punish its people for rebelling against their control. A year later, fighting broke out between Chinese and Soviet troops on the border between their two countries. Now, Mao and Zhou decided, was the time to draw closer to the Soviet Union's archenemy, the United States.

After careful preparations, U.S. president Richard Nixon visited Beijing in February 1972. The meeting that occurred between Nixon and Mao was historic, signaling China's new readiness to participate in international relations with noncommunist countries. China had also been able to replace Taiwan in the United Nations in 1971, a development previously resisted by the United States.

THE FOUR MODERNIZATIONS
The political climate within China seemed to

The Gang of Four: (from left) Zhang Chunqiao, Wang Hongwen, Yao Wenyuan, and Mao's wife Jiang Qing. After Mao's death, the four were arrested and found guilty of treason.

be changing. In 1975, Zhou Enlai launched a new program to reform the economy. Called the "Four Modernizations," it aimed to develop technology, agriculture, industry, science, and defense. Deng Xiaoping, who had been reinstated to the CCP in 1973, after his purge five years earlier, played an important part in formulating these new policies.

The tensions between unbending Marxists and practical politicians like Zhou Enlai had not disappeared, however. Despite his poor health—by now he could barely breathe—Mao still spoke out fiercely against "capitalist roaders." Meanwhile, his wife Jiang Qing and three associates, collectively known as the Gang of Four, were stirring up opposition to the Prime Minister and trying to revive Cultural Revolution policies.

THE DEATH OF ZHOU ENLAI
In January 1976, before the tensions could explode once more into violence, Zhou Enlai died of cancer. Mao, who had admired Zhou's political abilities but not his unorthodox Marxism, tried to suppress public mourning. People were not allowed even to

Zhou Enlai in 1975. A friend of Mao's from long before the Communists gained power, his political career lasted as long as Mao's.

Mao's body was embalmed after his death. It lies today in a mausoleum on Tiananmen Square that was opened to the public in 1977.

file past Zhou's coffin. Mao also moved against "rightists" within the CCP by failing to make the moderate Deng Xiaoping Zhou's successor, as had been expected. Instead, the job went to the more neutral Hua Guofeng, who became Chairman of the Communist Party when Mao died.

The Chinese Festival of the Dead, called Qingming, takes place in early April. As it approached, people responded to Mao's treatment of Zhou Enlai by laying wreaths in Beijing's Tiananmen Square and putting up posters declaring their affection for the late Prime Minister. During the night between April 4 and April 5, with Mao's approval, both the wreaths and posters were removed. The next day, thousands of people protested.

MAO'S FINAL DAYS

Mao Zedong's last major political act was to blame Deng Xiaoping for the unrest and dismiss him. In May, Mao suffered a minor heart attack. A second followed in June. Mao lived through the summer, urging colleagues to hold to his Marxist vision. On September 2, a final heart attack occurred. A week later, on September 9, 1976, Mao Zedong died.

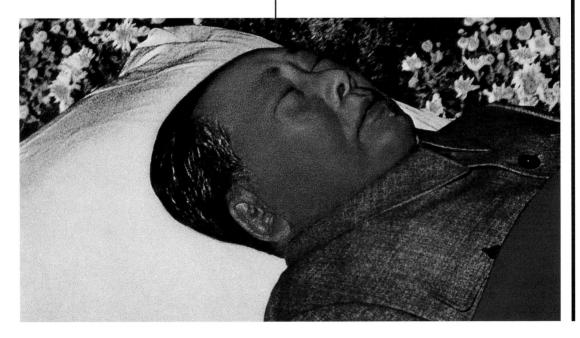

AGRICULTURAL REFORM – SUCCESS OR FAILURE?

Like about 94 percent of the Chinese population in the late 19th century, Mao Zedong was born a peasant. He knew from experience that most peasants lived in poverty and ignorance, at the mercy of natural disasters and their landlords. But after Mao had become the leader of China, did his grand schemes of land reform and collectivization really improve peasants' lives or even increase their crop yields? In other words, were they a success or a failure? Read both sides of the argument and the sources in the sidebars, and then judge for yourself.

SUCCESS?

SOURCE 1

PEASANT TYPE	% OF RURAL POPULATION	% OF LAND OWNED
POOR	60	18
MIDDLE	30	33
RICH AND LANDLORDS	10	49

FIGURES ARE AN AVERAGE FOR CHINA'S RURAL AREAS IN 1936

SOURCE 2

We are peasants, and so we want to unite with others who cultivate the land like we do . . . The interests of us who cultivate the land can only be protected by ourselves! . . . How do the landlords treat us? Are the rents and taxes heavy or light? Are our houses satisfactory or not? Are our bellies full or not? Is there enough land? Are there those in the village who have no land to cultivate? We must constantly seek answers to all these questions.
(EXTRACT FROM "THE GREAT UNION OF THE POPULAR MASSES" ARTICLES IN THE *XIANG RIVER REVIEW*, JULY/AUGUST 1919)

PEASANT TYPES

In Mao's time, there were many types of peasant. The poorest owned very little or no land, and middle peasants had enough land to grow their own food. The richest had spare land they could rent out. There were also many absentee landlords, who owned a good deal of the land that the poor farmed. All over China, rich peasants and landlords were a small part of the rural population, but they owned most of the land (*Source 1*).

PEASANT PROBLEMS

Peasants faced many problems. The most obvious was a shortage of land. Although China covers about 3.7 million square miles (9.6 million sq km), only about half a million (1.4 million) are suitable for farming. The good land had to be shared among a huge population. A typical peasant's southern farm covered less than 1.2 acres (0.5 hectare). Droughts, floods, and plagues of locusts often devastated crops.

Rice farmers at work in southern China.

CHINA'S LANDLORDS

Poor peasants suffered at the hands of rich peasants and landlords, both of whom charged exorbitant rents. In times of famine, landowners also took crops from villages in which people were starving and sold them for high prices in nearby

cities. As a young man, Mao already knew of peasants' troubles and urged them to unite to overcome them (*Source 2*).

LAND REFORM

Mao began to introduce land reform—the redistribution of land from landlords to poor peasants—in the 1920s. He started land reform in earnest in the late 1940s, as the Communists swept into power (*Source 3*). In 1950, the Agrarian Reform Law introduced a legal framework for the transfer of land from rich to poor (*Source 4*).

FARMING COOPERATIVES

Land reform was a success—after the new law had been implemented, poor peasants owned 46.8 percent of the land and landlords just 2.1 percent. Still, many poor people had to rent land from those who were richer. Mao was determined to end this inequality, so in the first Five Year-Plan, he created Mutual Aid Teams and, later, co-operatives. He hoped eventually to ensure that all land was commonly owned.

A cheery propaganda image of a women's Mutual Aid Team.

COMMUNE CULTURE

During the Great Leap Forward, Mao turned his attention to agriculture. Peasants on the huge new communes were told to increase crop yields and build irrigation networks. Poor management, floods, and droughts led to major problems; many communes had to be subdivided. But the farming and building work of these years laid the foundations for eventual increases in both output and cultivable land (*Source 5*).

LONG-TERM SUCCESS

Mao's land reform policies transformed land ownership in China. They also deprived landlords of their political power, allowing peasants to become a driving force for change. Mao's efforts to improve agriculture did not have the same instant success. Despite the upheavals of the Great Leap Forward, however, the long-term trends were good.

SOURCE 3

Later, in the year 1949, everything was settled about my land in Liu Ling. I was given a stamped certificate and everything. . . . It was the first land we had owned. No one had cultivated it before. We were very happy. Before that we never even dreamed of having our own land. Why should we? We didn't dream of anything . . . But now that we had got land of our own, Father came to me and said: "You should be grateful to the Communists. Without them you would never have got this land." (EXTRACT FROM *REPORT FROM A CHINESE VILLAGE* BY JAN MYRDAL)

SOURCE 4

Article 1. *The land ownership system of feudal exploitation by the landlord class shall be abolished and the system of peasant land ownership shall be carried into effect in order to set free the rural productive forces, develop agricultural production and pave the way for the industrialization of the new China.* (EXTRACT FROM THE AGRARIAN REFORM LAW OF JUNE 30, 1950)

SOURCE 5

	1949	1974
CULTIVATED LANDS	247	314 (MILLIONS OF ACRES)
IRRIGATED LANDS	49	99 (MILLIONS OF ACRES)
PRODUCTION OF GRAINS AND CEREALS	119	303 (MILLIONS OF TONS)

AGRICULTURAL REFORM – SUCCESS OR FAILURE?

FAILURE?

SOURCE 6

As the flames began to lick around his body Jin [a rich and powerful landlord] clenched his teeth, and did not utter even a moan until the fire surrounded his heart. The Communist officials sent to carry out the execution did not prevent the villagers from doing this. Although the Communists were opposed to torture in principle, officials were told that they should not intervene if the peasants wished to vent their anger in passionate acts of revenge.
(EXTRACT FROM THE AUTOBIOGRAPHY *WILD SWANS* BY JUNG CHANG)

SOURCE 7

A new upsurge in the socialist mass movement is imminent throughout the countryside. But some of our comrades are tottering along like a woman with bound feet and constantly complaining, "You're going too fast." Excessive criticism, inappropriate complaints, endless anxiety, and the erection of countless taboos—they believe this is the proper way to guide the socialist mass movement in the rural areas. No, this is not the right way; it is the wrong way.
(EXTRACT FROM "ON THE QUESTION OF AGRICULTURAL CO-OPERATION" BY MAO ZEDONG, JULY 31, 1955)

VISION AND REALITY

Mao Zedong's commitment to transforming the lives of China's peasants through land reform and agricultural improvement cannot be doubted. However, his extreme methods served only to increase rural problems.

LAND REFORM

As Communist land reform began in the 1950s, mass violence broke out in villages and thousands of landlords were killed, some burned alive (*Source 6*). The Agrarian Reform Law of 1950 tried to introduce a more orderly system of justice, but the brutality worsened. The law also failed in other ways. Although landlords were dispossessed, rich peasants were allowed to keep some of their land. Soon they were renting land to the poor just as landlords had done before them.

Jung Chang, the author of *Wild Swans*, now lives in London.

COOPERATIVE AGRICULTURE

In the first Five-Year Plan, Mao set out to prevent the growth of another class system by introducing cooperative agriculture. Many peasants resisted this move towards common ownership. They did not want to lose their new land and some had even begun to buy others' properties. Mao condemned this "spontaneous capitalism," as well as complaints about collectivization (*Source 7*), which he wanted to accelerate. There were practical as well as political reasons for Mao's

wish to advance collectivization. Farm profits were needed to fund industry (*Source 4*), but outputs were growing too slowly. Despite warnings about the dangers of bad planning, Mao decided the solution was to go faster.

THE GREAT LEAP FORWARD

Mao's determination led to the Great Leap Forward, which began in 1958. Central to this plan was the establishment of huge communes. These communes, however, were harmed by poor management and unrealistic goals (*Source 8*). The withdrawal of Soviet aid in 1960, as well as floods and droughts, made worse the problems of low output (*Source 9*) and famine.

Peasants building a flood barrier in 1958 during the Great Leap Forward.

AFTER THE GREAT LEAP

After 1959, many Great Leap policies were reversed. For example, between 1959 and 1960, average commune size was reduced by a third and much private land was restored to its original owners. Recovery was disrupted in the 1960s by the Mao-inspired Cultural Revolution, when political upheaval led to another slump in production (*Source 9*). Later, the Four Modernizations program, announced in 1975 by Zhou Enlai, was introduced to spur growth in agriculture, among other areas.

FARMING FAILURE

Mao pursued his political ideals in the countryside at the expense of China's peasants. The programs he pushed through, often against opposition from both Party members and the peasants themselves, led only to declining outputs and chaos. The Great Leap Forward, in particular, was a spectacular failure. It was only because of the intervention of less hard-line politicians that Chinese agriculture was able to recover. But even now, production figures are often exaggerated so that it remains difficult to assess the true situation (*Source 10*).

SOURCE 8

It was a time when telling fantasies to oneself as well as others, and believing them, was practised to an incredible degree. Peasants moved crops from several plots of land to one plot to show Party officials that they had produced a miracle harvest. Similar [fields] were shown off to gullible—or self-blinded—agricultural scientists, reporters, visitors from other regions, and foreigners.
(SECOND EXTRACT FROM THE AUTOBIOGRAPHY *WILD SWANS* BY JUNG CHANG)

SOURCE 9

PRODUCTION OF GRAINS

(MILLIONS OF TONS)

1957	325
1960	158
1967	209
1968	198

SOURCE 10

Many officials routinely make up production numbers to please their superiors, just as their predecessors did four decades ago during Chairman Mao Zedong's disastrous Great Leap Forward. . . . In June [1999], reporters of the official Xinhua news agency found some nearby townships and villages had already compiled their month-by-month statistics for 1999, which added up neatly to 101 per cent of the planned target.
(EXTRACT FROM 1999 INTERNET REPORT BY LATELINENEWS.COM)

INDUSTRIAL REFORM – SUCCESS OR FAILURE?

When Mao came to power in 1949, China's industrial output accounted for only about 10 percent of national production. Agriculture was far more important. The country's new leader, however, was determined first to equal and then to overtake the industrial output of major Western nations such as the United States and Britain. But were his efforts in this field a success? Or did Mao's insistence on political purity lead to failure? Read both sides of the argument and the sources, then judge for yourself.

SUCCESS?

Shanghai in 1926

GROWTH AND DECLINE

In the early 1900s, when Mao was growing up, industries such as mining and textile-making were developing in China, especially in the northeast and Shanghai. The civil war and the Japanese occupation, however, brought their decline. In 1949, the Communists had to rebuild before they could expand.

SOURCE 1

	COAL	STEEL
	(ESTIMATED OUTPUT IN TONS)	
1949	35,738,000	174,000
1952	73,272,000	1,488,000
1957	143,000,000	5,951,000

MAKING A START

From 1949 to 1952, the Chinese government was able to take control of most heavy industry because many of its owners were Nationalists who had fled to Taiwan. Output then began to rise (*Source 1*). Most light industry was run by ordinary businesspeople. Many remained in control until 1955, when the state takeover of private businesses began.

SOURCE 2

We shall have to master what we do not know. We must learn to do economic work from all who know how, no matter who they are. . . . We must acknowledge our ignorance, and not pretend to know what we do not know.
(EXTRACT FROM "ON THE PEOPLE'S DEMOCRATIC DICTATORSHIP" BY MAO ZEDONG, JUNE 30, 1949)

THE FIVE-YEAR PLAN

By 1953, postwar reconstruction was complete, and Mao was ready to introduce the Five-Year Plan. This plan set out to increase industrial production in China by 14.7 percent a year. At its heart was a scheme to develop 694 mines, steel factories, and other major projects. The Soviets were to provide financial and technical aid—Mao had always accepted the need for this help (*Source 2*)—and run about 140 plants.

STRIKING ACHIEVEMENT

The industrial aspect of the Five-Year Plan was a striking success. By 1957, Chinese production of many commodities,

including steel and coal (*Source 1*), had grown greatly. The overall increase in industrial output was about 15.5 percent a year. Many new products, including electrical goods, were being manufactured in China for the first time.

THE GREAT LEAP FORWARD

During the Great Leap Forward, Mao set out to accelerate industrial development. Steel production, in particular, was to reach 11.8 million tons in 1958 (*Source 3*) and 110 million tons by 1962. Ninety million people in the new communes participated in this program by building and running furnaces (*Source 4*). By 1960, steel production had indeed greatly increased (*Source 10*).

AFTER THE GREAT LEAP

Despite Mao's intentions, the Great Leap Forward failed, and Soviet aid was withdrawn. There was further upheaval during the Cultural Revolution, when protests disrupted factories. But in 1969, a more moderate program was introduced under the slogan "Promote Revolution, Grasp Production." Industry then grew at about 12 per cent a year. Consumer goods became important products and trade with the West increased. Zhou Enlai's Four Modernizations program of 1975 encouraged these upward trends to continue (*Source 5*).

Both men and women worked in Communist steel factories.

INDUSTRIAL SUCCESS

As a whole, Mao's industry policies were a great success. When he came to power, China was a largely agricultural country whose peasants had no industrial expertise. By 1978—only two years after his death—it had a growing industrial sector that produced 72 percent of the country's national output.

INDUSTRIAL REFORM – SUCCESS OR FAILURE?

FAILURE?

SOURCE 6

Communists must . . . combine the leadership with the masses . . . all correct leadership is necessarily 'from the masses, to the masses'. This means: take the ideas of the masses (scattered and unsystematic ideas) and concentrate them (through study turn them into concentrated and systematic ideas), then go to the masses and propagate and explain these ideas until the masses embrace them as their own.
(FROM A SPEECH BY MAO ZEDONG, 1967)

SOURCE 7

A climate of raw terror developed. Minor offenders, Mao declared, should be criticised and reformed, or sent to labour camps, while 'the worst among them should be shot'. For many, the psychological pressure became unbearable. The two campaigns together took several thousand . . . lives, the great majority by suicide, while an estimated 2 billion US dollars . . . was collected from private companies in fines for illicit activities.
(EXTRACT FROM *MAO: A LIFE* BY PHILIP SHORT)

MIXED MOTIVES

Mao's wish to improve China's industry was driven in part by a desire to strengthen the economy. But he also had political aims. He wanted to show that a Communist state could outdo Western capitalist countries. And he wanted to prove that his belief in the "mass line," the idea that the masses should both adopt and guide Communist practice (*Source 6*), was right. Industry often suffered as a result of these mixed motives.

THE "ANTIS" CAMPAIGNS

The early years of the Mao era brought a great increase in industrial output. But the 1951 launch of the Three and Five Antis Campaigns against financial crimes also provoked upheaval in the business community. The campaigns' main targets were factory-owners, whom Mao wanted to toe the Communist line. CCP teams were sent out to spy on and punish them. The results were disastrous (*Source 7*).

"Modern" Chinese factories still used mule-drawn carts.

THE FIVE-YEAR PLAN

Mao's insistence on the central importance of political aims also influenced the Five-Year Plan. To carry out their Five-Year Plans, the Soviets used many technicians who were not enthusiastic about Communism. But Mao said all scientists employed in China should be "Red as well as Expert." Other more practical CCP members, including Prime Minister Zhou Enlai, wanted to build industry quickly and worry about politics later.

THE GREAT LEAP FORWARD

Mao's political ideals affected industry most strongly during the Great Leap Forward. A main aim of this second Five-Year Plan was to hand power back to the people. In Mao's view, the first plan had been controlled too firmly by the CCP leadership. Under his new plan, peasants were to be far more active. Mass line politics—not economic necessity—was to be in command.

COMMUNE CHAOS

The result of this policy was the chaos of the communes. Peasants strove to achieve impossible feats without skills or materials. Even children scrambled to meet steel targets (*Source 8*), but much of the steel produced was not good enough to use. In 1959, Mao admitted that he had been misguided (*Source 9*), but it was too late to stop falls in steel and coal production (*Source 10*).

An unrealistically optimistic Great Leap Forward poster.

THE CULTURAL REVOLUTION AND AFTER

The Cultural Revolution that began in late 1965 was another attempt by Mao to enforce the mass line. Power was again to be wrenched from the center and returned to the people. The result was chaos once more as workers overthrew the "capitalist roaders" in factories. Calm returned to the country only after 1969, when Mao's ideas were set aside.

INDUSTRIAL FAILURE

Mao's political beliefs often clouded his economic judgment, with catastrophic results. If the ideals of the Great Leap Forward had continued to guide industry, China would have made little progress. Politicians with more flexible attitudes, such as Zhou Enlai, saved China from further disaster.

SOURCE 8

Every day, on my way to and from school, I screwed up my eyes to search every inch of ground for broken nails, rusty cogs, and any other metal objects that had been trodden into the mud between the cobbles. These were for feeding into furnaces to produce steel, which was my major occupation.
Yes, at the age of six, I was involved in steel production. . . .
(EXTRACT FROM THE AUTOBIOGRAPHY *WILD SWANS* BY JUNG CHANG)

SOURCE 9

Before August of last year my main energies were concentrated on revolution. I am a complete outsider when it comes to economic construction, and I understand nothing about industrial planning. . . . But comrades, in 1958 and 1959 the main responsibility was mine, and you should take me to task [criticize me].
(EXTRACT FROM A 1959 SPEECH BY MAO ZEDONG)

SOURCE 10

	STEEL	COAL
	(ESTIMATED OUTPUT IN TONS)	
1959	11,000,000	320,000,000
1960	14,000,000	297,000,000
1961	9,000,000	198,000,000

EDUCATION FOR ALL – REALITY OR ILLUSION?

Until the Communist takeover in 1949, the great majority of China's population—between 80 and 90 percent—had received no education and could neither read nor write. Like Mao Zedong, children whose parents could afford to send them to school studied mainly Confucius and other Chinese classics. Once he was in power, Mao set out to shake up this outdated system and to bring education to all. But did he succeed, or did the Cultural Revolution that he inspired upset all his plans? Read both sides of the argument and the sources, then judge for yourself.

REALITY?

SOURCE 1

In the early morning I study English; from eight in the morning to three in the afternoon I attend class; from four . . . until dinner, I study Chinese literature; from the time the lights are lit until they are extinguished, I do homework . . . and after the lights are extinguished, I exercise for one hour.
(EXTRACT FROM MAO'S WRITINGS OF 1915)

SOURCE 2

In the educational system of our country, required courses are as thick as the hairs on a cow. Even an adult with a tough, strong body could not stand it, let alone those who have not reached adulthood.
(EXTRACT FROM MAO'S WRITINGS OF 1915)

SOURCE 3

	PRIMARY SCHOOL PUPILS	SECONDARY SCHOOL PUPILS
1949	24 MILLION	1 MILLION
1952	51 MILLION	2.5 MILLION

MAO'S BELIEFS

Mao Zedong firmly believed in the power of education to improve people's lives and was an extremely hard-working student himself (*Source 1*). However, he despised pure "book learning"—that is, elitist education irrelevant to ordinary life. He was also critical of the complex curriculum that young Chinese had to study (*Source 2*).

Children in a Shanghai classroom.

FIRST STEPS

Once in power, Mao introduced measures to bring education to the masses. For example, "winter schools" were opened where people could study during the cold months when there was little work in the fields. In addition, literacy classes were set up in factories and city slums. More children were also encouraged to attend school and attendance rose (*Source 3*).

THE FIVE-YEAR PLAN

During the Five-Year Plan, the pace of change increased. Many more primary and middle schools opened, and the number of students attending these schools and China's universities increased. In 1955, the government produced a code of conduct for students (*Source 4*). By 1957, China had 64 million primary-school pupils. The same year 56,000 people graduated from the country's universities, compared with 48,000 in 1953.

THE GREAT LEAP FORWARD

In January 1958, as the Great Leap Forward began, Mao took several steps to break down barriers between intellectuals and peasants. In particular, he established work-study groups where peasants could learn subjects such as philosophy and painting, as well as industrial skills and basic literacy. At the same time, Mao organized national propaganda campaigns designed to teach intellectuals that peasants were their equals.

THE CULTURAL REVOLUTION

It was, however, through the Cultural Revolution that Mao shook up China's education system most radically. In a 1966 decision, the CCP leadership explained exactly how it wished to reform teaching (*Source 5*). By then, the Red Guards were already criticizing teachers for their revisionist ways. As the protests grew, schools and universities closed. Many students went to the country to "learn from the peasants."

EDUCATION IN THE 1970s

Mao talking to a Tianjin university student learning to operate industrial machinery.

Once the Cultural Revolution was over, educational institutions began to reopen. But it was no longer acceptable for them to be set apart from the world of work. All students who wished to enter higher education were required to first do two years of industrial or agricultural work, and both school and university courses were restructured to include various forms of manual work (*Source 6*).

REVOLUTIONARY REALITY

In the field of education, Mao put his principles into practice. He gave millions of peasants the opportunity to learn reading, writing, and more for the first time. By 1971, China's literacy rate had soared to 90 percent. At the same time, in accordance with his Marxist principles, Mao ensured that intellectuals learned about the lives of ordinary workers.

SOURCE 4

1. Endeavor to be a good student; good in health, good at study and good in conduct. Prepare to serve the Motherland and the people. . . .
3. Obey all the instructions of the principal and teachers. Value and protect the reputation of the school and of the class. . . .
(EXTRACT FROM "RULES OF CONDUCT FOR STUDENTS," PREPARED BY THE CHINESE MINISTRY OF EDUCATION, 1955)

SOURCE 5

It is imperative to carry out the policy . . . of making education serve proletarian politics and having education integrated with productive labor. . . . The academic course must be shortened and the curriculum simplified. . . . Besides studying academic subjects, [students] should also learn to do industrial, agricultural and military work.
(EXTRACT FROM THE ELEVENTH PLENUM'S DECISION, AUGUST 8, 1966)

SOURCE 6

You wonder at first if you are on a campus at all. Here at Communications University (C.U.) in Sian are people, dressed in conical hats and blue peasant jackets, threshing wheat. . . . In the Middle School attached to Beijing Normal University, girls are making chairs. Next door are boys . . . making semiconductors.
(EXTRACT FROM 800,000,000: THE REAL CHINA BY ROSS TERRILL)

EDUCATION FOR ALL – REALITY OR ILLUSION?

ILLUSION?

SOURCE 7

All secondary schools . . . should, if possible, experiment in setting up workshops and farms to attain complete or partial self-sufficiency by engaging in production. Students should do part-time study and part-time work. . . . The middle and primary schools of a village should sign contracts with local co-operatives to take part in agricultural . . . production.
(EXTRACT FROM "SIXTY POINTS ON WORK METHODS," BY MAO ZEDONG, 1958)

SOURCE 8

One day my mother bicycled to the school to find that the pupils had rounded up the headmaster, the academic supervisor, the graded teachers, whom they understood from the official press to be 'reactionary bourgeois authorities,' and any other teachers they disliked. They had shut them all up in a classroom and put a notice on the door saying 'demons' class'. The teachers had let them do it because the Cultural Revolution had thrown them into bewilderment.
(EXTRACT FROM THE AUTOBIOGRAPHY *WILD SWANS* BY JUNG CHANG)

POLICY PROBLEMS

Mao undoubtedly wished to open up education to all the people of China. Many of the policies that he devised to achieve this aim, however, were seriously flawed. In addition, some caused so much disruption that they actually reduced students' chances of getting a good education.

FIVE-YEAR PLAN FLAWS

The achievements of the Five-Year Plan in the field of education were marred by many problems. In particular, although more students enrolled in schools and universities, many never finished their programs. In senior middle schools, 98 percent of pupils failed to complete their educations. At the university level, this number rose to 99 percent. As a result, there were serious shortages of scientists and other specialists in China.

EDUCATIONAL INEQUALITIES

The Five-Year Plan ignored other problems, too. In particular, it failed to set up any institutions of higher education in rural areas, where there were none. It also did nothing to improve educational opportunities for girls and young women; there were twice as many boys than girls in China's primary schools, and three times as many in its universities.

"Antirevolutionary" teachers were often forced to wear dunce caps.

THE GREAT LEAP FORWARD

Because Mao insisted that they should not spend all their time studying but also take on other work (*Source 7*), the Great Leap Forward disrupted the education of millions of young people. In 1958 and 1959, about 3 million secondary school and university students were sent to labor on

building sites and farms in order to learn from the workers.
A million teachers and other intellectuals had to do the same.

THE CULTURAL REVOLUTION

Matters grew far worse during the Cultural Revolution. While
schools and universities were still open, pupils humiliated,
beat, and even killed teachers (*Source 8*). Most educational
institutions, however, were closed in 1966 (*Source 9*). Schools
began to reopen in 1968. Universities reopened in 1970.
Millions missed years of education. Later surveys of literacy
showed that many people never made up their lost schooling.

STUDY IN THE '70s

The Cultural Revolution led to changes in education that
endured until the end of the Mao era. In particular, courses
were shortened so that there would be more time
for students to do manual work. It was, of
course, impossible to learn the same
amount when study time and material
had been cut, so learning suffered
(*Source 10*). Another change was that only
applicants with strict Maoist political views
were accepted to universities. As a result,
university enrollments decreased significantly
(*Source 11*).

These Shanghai students had to clear up sewage as well as study.

EDUCATIONAL ILLUSION

Mao's good intentions in the field of education
came to very little. The excesses of the Great Leap
Forward and the Cultural
Revolution wiped out early gains. After Mao's death in 1976,
China's leaders restored old curricula and stopped making
students work in factories and on farms. They realized that
Mao had destroyed his own vision of education for all.

SOURCE 9

*Considering that the Great
Cultural Revolution is only
now developing in the
colleges, universities and
senior middle schools, a
certain period of time
will be needed to carry
this movement through
thoroughly and
successfully. Bourgeois
domination is still deeply
rooted and the struggle
between the proletariat
and the bourgeois is very
acute. . . .*
(EXTRACT FROM CCP DECISION
TO SUSPEND HIGHER EDUCATION,
JUNE 13, 1966)

SOURCE 10

*One distinguished scientist,
. . . discussed this matter of
shortened courses around
and around. Yet I still felt
puzzled about how, at his
university, five years'
scientific training could
be put into two and a
half. Our last meeting was
at Peking Airport. . . . He
concluded on a note he
had not struck before: "I
was not myself opposed
to keeping the five-year
course, Now, well now, we
just have to work out what
we can realistically omit."*
(EXTRACT FROM 800,000,000:
THE REAL CHINA BY ROSS
TERRILL)

SOURCE 11

STUDENT NUMBERS BEFORE AND AFTER CULTURAL REVOLUTION		
	BEFORE	AFTER
BEIJING UNIVERSITY	9,000	2,667
FU TAN UNIVERSITY, SHANGHAI	9,000	1,196

JUDGE FOR YOURSELF

TRANSFORMATION OR TRADITION—DID MAO CHANGE WOMEN'S LIVES?

In traditional Chinese society, which was guided by Confucian thought, women were considered inferior to men. Even as a very young man, however, Mao rebelled against this idea and advocated the equality of the sexes. Later, when he came to power, the first major piece of legislation he passed was the 1950 Marriage Law. But in the long term, did Mao's Communist regime really transform the lives of women, or were the old traditions too strong to overcome? Read both sides of the argument and the sources, then judge for yourself.

TRANSFORMATION?

SOURCE 1

Gentlemen, we are women! . . . We are also human beings . . . [yet] we are not even allowed to go outside the front gate. The shameless men, the villainous men, make us into their playthings. . . . But so-called 'chastity' is confined to us women! The 'temples to virtuous women' are scattered all over the place, but where are the 'pagodas to chaste men'?
(EXTRACT FROM "THE GREAT UNION OF THE POPULAR MASSES" ARTICLES IN THE *XIANG RIVER REVIEW*, JULY/AUGUST 1919)

SOURCE 2

Yesterday's incident was important. It happened because of the shameful system of arranged marriages, because of the darkness of the social system, the negation of the individual will, and the absence of the freedom to choose one's own mate.
(EXTRACT FROM "MISS ZHAO'S SUICIDE," A NOVEMBER 1919 ARTICLE BY MAO ZEDONG)

EARLY IDEAS

Mao was a student of Confucius. He rejected, however, the Confucian idea of the "three bonds" between ruler and subject, father and son, and husband and wife. He thought people should choose their relationships, not be tied to others against their will. In the summer of 1919, Mao used one of the "Great Union of the Popular Masses" articles to act as a spokesperson for unhappily married women (*Source 1*).

MISS ZHAO

In another article that appeared in November 1919, Mao examined the case of Miss Zhao, a young woman who had killed herself rather than be forced to marry an older man she did not love. Again, Mao spoke up for the woman and against the traditional family system that had placed her in what he saw as an intolerable position (*Source 2*).

PRINCIPLE INTO PRACTICE

While the CCP was seeking power, its Women's Association organized campaigns against wife-beating and foot-binding, the ancient—and already illegal—practice of wrapping strips of cloth around young girls' feet to keep them small. But it was not

Foot-binding produced painful deformities.

until the People's Republic was founded that Mao could tackle the underlying problem of women's oppression. He did so in the Marriage Law, passed on May 1, 1950 (*Source 3*).

THE MARRIAGE LAW

A traditional wedding in 19th-century China.

The Marriage Law contained measures for the protection of women and children. Marriage was to be freely entered into by women as well as men. Children were to be properly cared for and raised. Infanticide was explicitly banned. This was an important provision, because in a society that considered them of little worth, baby girls were often killed. After the Marriage Law was passed, many women who had been forced into marriages divorced their husbands.

WOMEN AND WORK

As the Great Leap Forward was about to begin, Mao promoted the equality of women in another way. Mao pointed out that women should form a major part of the labor force that was setting out to strengthen China's agriculture and industry (*Source 4*). Soon many millions of women began to operate backyard furnaces, as well as cook in the communal canteens that fed other workers. They were able to do so because the communes had nurseries where they could leave their children.

BIRTH CONTROL

Mao's Communist Party also helped women by providing them with birth control. This policy was introduced in 1956, but then was abandoned during the Great Leap Forward, when the aim was to increase China's population. In 1960, Mao's government again began providing women with birth control, and this has since given women much greater control over their lives.

BETTER LIVES

During his time in power, Mao transformed women's lives. In particular, he freed them from forced marriages and unwanted pregnancies. He also gave them important new opportunities to work and to earn the same pay as men for their labor.

SOURCE 3

Article 1: *The arbitrary and compulsory feudal marriage system, which is based on the superiority of man over woman and which ignores the children's interests, shall be abolished.*

The New Democratic marriage system, which is based on free choice of partners, on monogamy, on equal rights for both sexes, and on protection of the lawful interests of women and children, shall be put into effect.
Article 2: *Bigamy, concubinage, child betrothal, interference with the remarriage of widows and the exaction of money or gifts in connection with marriage shall be prohibited.*
Article 13: *Parents have the duty to rear and to educate their children; the children have the duty to support and to assist their parents. Neither the parents nor the children shall maltreat or desert one another. . . . Infanticide by drowning and similar criminal acts is strictly prohibited.*
(EXTRACTS FROM THE MARRIAGE LAW OF MAY 1, 1950)

SOURCE 4

China's women are a vast reserve of labour power. This reserve should be tapped and used in the struggle to build a mighty socialist country. To encourage women to join in productive labour, we must put into effect the principle of equal pay for equal work, men and women alike. . . .
(EXTRACT FROM *SOCIALIST UPSURGE IN CHINA'S COUNTRYSIDE*, 1956)

TRANSFORMATION OR TRADITION—DID MAO CHANGE WOMEN'S LIVES?

TRADITION?

SOURCE 5

	% OF FULL MEMBERS OF THE CCP CENTRAL COMMITTEE WHO WERE WOMEN
1945	2
1956	4
1969	8
1973	10
1977	7

SOURCE 6

In the old society . . . the Confucian morality of the 'three obediences and the four virtues' and the 'three submissions and five rules' . . . . ruined the lives of countless unfortunate victims. This happened to my first cousin. . . . Her father had arranged a marriage for her, but as soon as the marriage was set, the husband died! But still she had to go through the ceremony of 'crossing the threshold' because from now on 'as long as you live you are a member of your in-laws' family, and when you are dead you will be a spirit of that family. . . .'
(EXTRACT FROM A DOCUMENT IN WHICH THE WOMEN OF SHAOXING DISTRICT CRITICIZE CONFUCIUS, 1974)

FIGHTING PREJUDICE

Mao Zedong definitely set out to free women from the bonds of prejudice and tradition that had always blighted their lives. It proved impossible, however, to turn his grand visions into reality. Furthermore, in his own personal life, Mao often failed to show women care and respect.

PARTY WOMEN

In the early years of the CCP, Mao and his male colleagues did not treat women as equals. In the mountain base areas, most female party members spent their time carrying out traditional women's tasks, such as cooking and sewing. This may have been their choice, but, in any case, a greater role in the revolution was not open to them. Later, few women were members of the CCP Central Committee (*Source 5*).

THE MARRIAGE LAW

The 1950 Marriage Law was a groundbreaking piece of legislation. However, it was disregarded by many men, who still treated women exactly as before. Other outlawed practices also continued, included the payment of bride prices and the killing of female children. The Communists could have mounted a campaign to make people obey the law, but failed to do so. This was probably because they did not want to upset the peasant masses on whom they depended for support.

Women building roads alongside men in Hubei.

MARRIAGE MISTREATMENT

The Marriage Law failed to address one major problem. When Chinese peasant women marry, they have to leave their home villages and go to their husbands' villages. There, they are always regarded as strangers and often mistreated by their in-laws. Under Mao, the CCP did little to support women who campaigned against this form of abuse.

WOMEN AND WORK

Despite Mao's efforts, women also had problems at work. The men who ran the collectives set up by the first Five-Year Plan rarely let women rise to positions of power. In the communes created during the Great Leap Forward, some women became leaders of teams in their brigades. Even by the 1970s, however, women never made up more than 21 percent of the leaders.

CRITICIZING CONFUCIUS

The fact that women in China were still oppressed in the 1970s is proven by their participation in the movement to criticize Confucius. Part of the Cultural Revolution, this movement involved speaking out against the traditional ways that Confucius praised. Women used the movement to protest against the custom of having to move to a new village upon marriage (*Source 6*).

MAO'S WOMEN

Mao did not treat his first three wives well (*Source 7*). He also grew apart from his fourth, Jiang Qing. Although they never divorced, in his final years Mao had a succession of young female companions. Jiang eventually killed herself in jail.

TRADITIONAL TIES

Mao attempted to improve the lives of China's women, especially by introducing the Marriage Law. Many Chinese, however, clung to tradition and were slow to adopt the ideas he promoted. Often, he was not faithful to them himself.

SOURCE 7

The women who shared Mao's life all had their part of misfortune. Miss Luo, the peasant girl his parents chose, suffered the disgrace of rejection and died an early death. Yang Kaihui went to the execution ground proclaiming her loyalty to him, but spiritually crushed by the knowledge that he was living with He Zizhen. She, in her turn, endured extraordinary hardship . . . sharing Mao's lot in the darkest periods of his political career only to find that, when finally they were able to live normally again, they had grown apart.
(EXTRACT FROM *MAO: A LIFE* BY PHILIP SHORT)

Jiang Qing under arrest in 1981.

MAO'S FOREIGN POLICY—PRINCIPLED OR PRACTICAL?

From ancient times, China thought of itself as the Middle Kingdom, a superior nation at the center of the globe. As a result, it generally kept its distance from the rest of the world. But in the 19th century, it was eventually forced to accept contact and trade with the West. From 1949, Mao Zedong had to decide how the new People's Republic was going to relate to other countries. But was his foreign policy based on the strict Marxist principles he often promoted or did he simply adopt a practical approach, doing whatever seemed best for China? Read both sides of the argument and the sources, then judge for yourself.

PRINCIPLED?

SOURCE 1

Externally, unite in a common struggle with those nations of the world which treat us as equals and with the peoples of all countries. That is, ally ourselves with the Soviet Union, with the People's Democracies and with the proletariat and the broad masses of the people in all other countries, and form an international united front.
(EXTRACT FROM "ON THE PEOPLE'S DEMOCRATIC DICTATORSHIP" BY MAO ZEDONG, JUNE 30, 1949)

SOURCE 2

The Soviet Union and China undertake . . . to develop and consolidate economic and cultural ties between the Soviet Union and China, to render each other every possible economic assistance, and to carry out the necessary economic co-operation.
(EXTRACT FROM THE TREATY OF FRIENDSHIP, ALLIANCE AND MUTUAL ASSISTANCE BETWEEN THE SOVIET UNION AND THE PEOPLE'S REPUBLIC OF CHINA, FEBRUARY 14, 1950)

MAKING A START

Mao made clear even before he came to power that he intended to build foreign-policy alliances with Communist countries such as the Soviet Union, but not with governments of "imperialist" countries such as the United States (*Source 1*). In 1950, a formal treaty was signed with the Soviet Union (*Source 2*).

CHINA AND THE UNITED STATES

Mao's Marxist principles led him to regard the United States as China's archenemy. First, it was the world's foremost capitalist nation and strongly anti-Communist. Second, it had supported the Nationalists in the civil war. Third, it refused to recognize China's Communist government, blocking its membership in the United Nations.

KOREAN AND VIETNAM WARS

Mao put his foreign-policy principles into practice during the Korean War. After Communist North Korean troops invaded non-Communist South Korea in 1950, a United Nations force made up largely of soldiers from the United States opposed them.

Propaganda image of Chinese troops capturing American tanks in Korea.

The North Koreans had acted with full Soviet approval. But it was Mao who sent forces to support them. Some 400,000

58

Chinese died fighting the Korean War. Mao also supported Communist North Vietnam against non-Communist South Vietnam and the United States during the Vietnam War of 1954 to 1975 (*Source 3*). This time, however, Chinese aid mainly took the form of weapons and ammunition.

CHINA IN AFRICA

Mao also backed Communists in newly independent African nations such as the Democratic Republic of the Congo (formerly Zaire), where they struggled to seize power in the 1950s and 1960s. The supply of arms and military advisers again brought China into conflict with the United States. Sometimes it also caused tension with the Soviet Union, which provided support and aid to different groups.

A 1969 border dispute worsened tensions between China and the Soviet Union.

BREAK WITH THE SOVIET UNION

The split between China and the Soviet Union in the late 1950s was caused in part by Mao's disgust at what he saw as Soviet betrayal of Marxist principles. He disapproved strongly of Khrushchev's 1956 attack on Stalin (*Source 4*) and his decision to begin a policy of peaceful coexistence with the United States. Mao was also appalled by the Soviet Union's 1968 invasion of Czechoslovakia (*Source 5*).

FRIENDSHIP WITH THE UNITED STATES

In his final years, Mao drew closer to the United States, but only after certain conditions had been met. First, in 1969, U.S. President Nixon agreed to increase his efforts to withdraw U.S. troops from Vietnam. Second, in 1971, the U. S. was forced to accept China as a member of the United Nations.

A MATTER OF PRINCIPLE

Mao Zedong was as faithful to Marxism in his foreign policy as in his domestic policy. He never seriously wavered from his commitment to Communism, wherever it needed support.

SOURCE 3

The struggle of the Vietnamese people against U.S. aggression and for national salvation is now the focus of the struggle of the people of the world against U.S. aggression. . . . No matter what U.S. imperialism may do to expand its war adventure, the Chinese people will do everything in their power to support the Vietnamese people until every single one of the U.S. aggressors is driven out of Vietnam.
(EXTRACT FROM A SPEECH BY CHINESE DEFENCE MINISTER LIN BIAO, SEPTEMBER 3, 1965)

SOURCE 4

Some people consider that Stalin was wrong in everything: this is a grave misconception. . . . We should view Stalin from an historical standpoint, make a proper and all-round analysis to see where he was right and where he was wrong and draw useful lessons therefrom.
(EXTRACT FROM AN APRIL 1956 EDITORIAL IN THE *PEOPLE'S DAILY*, A NEWSPAPER THAT EXPRESSED THE VIEWS OF THE CCP)

SOURCE 5

After its flagrant armed occupation of Czechoslovakia with the tacit consent of US imperialism, the Soviet revisionist renegade clique has ruthlessly suppressed the Czechoslovak people by fascist means. . . .
(EXTRACT FROM THE CHINESE ENGLISH-LANGUAGE NEWSPAPER *BEIJING REVIEW*, SEPTEMBER 6, 1968)

MAO'S FOREIGN POLICY — PRINCIPLED OR PRACTICAL?

PRACTICAL?

SOURCE 6

. . . our nation will from now on enter the large family of peace-loving and freedom-loving nations of the world. It will work bravely to create its own civilization and happiness and will at the same time promote world peace and freedom. Our nation will never again be an insulted nation. We have stood up.
(EXTRACT FROM MAO ZEDONG'S SPEECH PROCLAIMING THE PEOPLE'S REPUBLIC OF CHINA, OCTOBER 1, 1949)

SOURCE 7

China's foreign relations . . . are a complex phenomenon made up of partially contradictory elements. At one extreme, we may encounter the pursuit of national interest . . . in a virtually pure form. At the other, we observe an effort to promote or encourage social revolution within individual foreign countries. . . . Between the two lies a no-man's land in which national and revolutionary motives are mingled.
(EXTRACT FROM *THE POLITICAL THOUGHT OF MAO TSE-TUNG* BY STUART R. SCHRAM)

PRACTICAL PRINCIPLES

When Mao came to power, he was determined that China would never again be bullied by the West or Japan (*Source 6*). He was also determined to rebuild his country after the civil war. As a result, he needed the Soviet Union's political, technical, and financial support. Although Marxist principles played a part in Mao's decision to ally with his Communist neighbor, there were also practical reasons for the alliance.

CHINA AND THE WEST

Even early in his rule, Mao was not opposed on principle to contact with the West. After Britain and other European countries recognized Communist China in the 1950s, he aimed to establish closer links with them. Chinese intervention in the Korean War made progress toward this goal impossible, but China made further attempts after the war's end. These were rebuffed by the United States and other nations, particularly those that opposed Mao's plans to seize Nationalist Taiwan.

Soviet tanks in Hungary in 1956.

THE KOREAN AND VIETNAM WARS

Despite his principles, Mao was not eager for China to participate in the Korean War. He resisted intervention on the side of North Korea for four months. Mao's relationship with Vietnam was not clear-cut, either. He knew that, in principle, he should back the North Vietnamese, but feared that a united, Communist Vietnam would threaten China. His commitment to world Communism, like his aid to Vietnam, had limits.

OPPOSING IMPERIALISM?

Although Mao opposed Western imperialism, he often argued that China had the right to influence and take over other countries. During the 1930s, he expressed

the wish that China should again have influence over states such as Burma, which had come under European control. Once in power, he reannexed Tibet and regularly meddled in the Third World. When the Soviet Union was still an ally, he sometimes backed Soviet imperialism. For example, Mao supported the 1956 invasion of Hungary, though he scorned the Soviet policies that made it necessary. In other words, Mao accepted imperialism when it was in China's interests (*Source 7*).

CHINA AND THE THIRD WORLD

Mao's support for Communist guerrillas in Africa and Asia was shaky. At first, he gave them military aid, but at the 1955 conference of Third World countries in Bandung, Indonesia, China only promised to give money to African governments. By the 1960s, China was helping guerrillas again, but they were not always Communists. In Angola, Mao backed an anti-Communist group in order to stop a Soviet-backed Communist group. Once more, Mao's principles proved flexible.

CHANGING SIDES

The clearest sign that Mao's foreign policy was not principled was China's new relationship with the non-Communist United States in the 1970s. This alliance enabled China to oppose the Soviet Union more effectively, but betrayed Mao's ideal of Communist solidarity (*Source 8*). The bulletin issued after U.S. President Nixon's 1972 visit committed China to peaceful relations with the United States (*Source 9*)— a policy for which Mao had condemned Khrushchev.

Mao's wife Jiang Qing chats to President Nixon during his China trip.

PRACTICAL POLITICS

In the realm of foreign policy, Mao Zedong was always prepared to compromise his Marxist principles. What drove him above all was the practical matter of China's survival in a hostile and ever-changing world.

SOURCE 8

In opening the door to America, Mao had responded to geopolitical necessity – the need for a common front to contain the expansionist impulses of Russia. The price had been the abandonment of his vision of a new Red 'Middle Kingdom' from which the world's revolutionaries would draw hope and inspiration. In its place came cold-eyed balance-of-power politics aimed at guaranteeing not revolution but survival.
(EXTRACT FROM *MAO: A LIFE* BY PHILIP SHORT)

SOURCE 9

. . . the two sides agree that countries, regardless of their social systems, should conduct their relations on the principles of respect for the sovereignty and territorial integrity of all states, nonaggression against other states, non-interference in the internal affairs of other states, equality and mutual benefit, and peaceful coexistence. International disputes should be settled on this basis, without resorting to the use or threat of force. The United States and the People's Republic of China are prepared to apply these principles to their mutual relations.
(EXTRACT FROM THE SHANGHAI COMMUNIQUÉ, FEBRUARY 27, 1972)

GLOSSARY

agrarian: of or relating to land, its ownership, or its cultivation.

Allies: the countries that fought together against Germany in World War I and World War II. In World War I, the main Allies were Britain, France, Russia, and the United States (from 1917), who were supported by China and Japan. In World War II, the main Allies were Britain, the Soviet Union, and the United States (from 1941); this time Japan, which invaded China was on the opposing side.

armistice: an official agreement between opposing sides to stop the fighting in a war.

bolshevism: Russian Communism; Bolsheviks were the radical members of the Russian Social Democratic Party who advocated revolution and took power in 1917.

bourgeois: in Marxist theory, favoring capitalism, and therefore hostile to the working class.

Boxer: a member of a secret society that opposed, and in 1900 rebelled unsuccessfully against, foreign influence in China. The English name "Boxer" is a rough translation of a Chinese name that literally means "righteous harmonious fist."

bride price: money or goods given by a groom to his future wife's family in order to "buy" his bride and rights over her.

capitalism: an economic system in which businesses are owned and run by private individuals for their own profit, rather than by the state.

capitalist: (noun) a person who supports capitalism or a person who owns one or more businesses for personal profit; (adjective) of or relating to capitalism.

cell: any one of the smallest units into which an organization is divided.

character: any of the approximately 2,000 symbols used to write the Chinese language. Chinese characters represent ideas, not sounds. They are pronounced in different ways in different parts of China.

coalition: a government containing members of more than one political party.

collective: (noun) a farm under the joint control of a large number of people rather than a single individual or family; (adjective) of, shared, or carried out by people acting together rather than individually.

Comintern: an international Communist organization that was established by Vladimir Lenin in Russia in 1919 and remained active until 1943. The name is short for "Communist International."

commune: any of the living units established by Mao Zedong during the Great Leap Forward (1958-1962) in which people did not live as individual families, instead sharing dormitories, dining rooms, and other facilities and working together in brigades.

communism: a political and economic system that aims to create a classless society. Communist countries are ruled by members of one political party, who are not elected. Businesses in such countries are owned by the state rather than by private individuals.

communist: (noun) a person who supports communism and who may also be a member of an official Communist Party; (adjective) of or relating to Communism.

counterrevolutionary: a revolutionary who tries to overthrow the government or ruling group established by a previous revolution.

courtyard house: a typical style of single-story Chinese house in which rooms are grouped around one or more open central courtyards.

despotism: rule by a person with absolute power, especially one who misuses that power; tyranny.

dynasty: a family that rules a country for generations.

feudalism: a political and social system in which a monarch owns all the land and loans it to nobles in return for military service. Nobles in turn loan land in return for services or goods to knights, knights to peasants, and so on. In this way, a hierarchy of rights and duties is established. Feudalism began in Europe during the 8th century A.D. and continued for centuries. Similar systems also operated in China and elsewhere.

Forbidden City: the Beijing palace complex built for China's emperors in the 15th century A.D. It contains 800 buildings, and is surrounded by a wall and moat, originally designed to keep ordinary people out.

geopolitical: relating to the influence of geographical factors—for example, a country's position, the size of its population or the nature of its industries—on politics.

guerrilla warfare: a type of warfare used by members of small, unofficial, and often politically inspired fighting units to attack larger armies. Guerrilla soldiers, also known as guerrillas, are highly mobile and specialize in surprise attacks and sabotage, rather than major battles.

Han dynasty: the dynasty that ruled China from 206 B.C.–A.D. 220. The Han emperors both strengthened the country and expanded its territory. Mao was a great admirer of the fifth Han emperor, Han Wudi.

imperialism: the policy or practice of extending a country's power, especially by taking over territories beyond its borders or acquiring indirect control over foreign governments.

Industrial Revolution: the historical period during which change from a largely agricultural economy, based on crop-growing and animal-rearing, to a largely industrial economy, based on the production of goods in factories, took place. This change began in Britain in the mid-18th century and by the late 19th century had spread to the rest of Europe, the United States, and beyond.

Kuomintang: the Chinese Nationalist Party, founded by Sun Yat-sen in 1912. The name literally means "National People's Party."

Manchu: a member of a nomadic people from the region of Manchuria, now in northeast China, who conquered the Chinese in 1644. The Manchus founded the Qing dynasty.

manifesto: a statement of beliefs, aims, and policies published by a political organization or another type of organization.

opium: a powerful and addictive drug made from the unripe seeds of the opium poppy, a type of plant.

plenum: an assembly of all members of an organization, especially a legislative body.

politburo: the main policy-making body of a communist party; the word is a short form of the Russian word meaning "political bureau."

proletariat: in Marxist theory, the wage-earning industrial or other workers who own no land and must therefore sell their labor to business-owning capitalists in order make a living.

propaganda: ideas, facts, or rumors spread in order to help one's own political cause or to harm the cause of another.

protectorate: a state or other territory that is under the control of, but not annexed to, another, more powerful state.

puppet state: a nation that is officially independent but is under the control of another, more powerful state.

purge: (verb) to expel, as from a political party or other body); (noun) an expulsion of members regarded as treacherous or disloyal.

Qin dynasty: the dynasty that unified China and then ruled the country from 221–207 B.C. Mao was a great admirer of the first Qin emperor, Qin Shihuangdi.

Qing dynasty: the dynasty of Manchus that ruled China from 1644 to 1912 and was overthrown by Sun Yat-sen's Nationalists.

Qingming: the Chinese Festival of the Dead, which occurs in early April. During the festival, people visit their relatives' graves, clean them, and sometimes also leave flowers; "Qingming" literally means "tomb sweep." Some people also burn "ghost money" on the graves so that their ancestors can spend it in the afterlife.

Red Army: the Chinese Communist army that was led by Zhu De and later became known as the People's Liberation Army. (The army of the Soviet Union was also known as the Red Army.)

renegade: a traitorous person or organization.

republic: a country or other political unit with elected rulers and no emperor, king, or queen.

revisionism: in Marxist theory, the belief that the communist movement should turn away from trying to bring about a communist society through revolution and, instead, adopt an evolutionary approach.

rightist: a person who supports conservative, or "right-wing," political ideals that are in opposition to Communist political ideals.

Russian Revolution: the revolution that took place in Russia in 1917 that resulted in the overthrow of the imperial Romanov family and the establishment of a Communist government led by Vladimir Lenin.

Soviet: (often capitalized) a) a local, regional, or national council run according to Communist principles. The name was originally used in the USSR (Union of Soviet Socialist Republics); b) a citizen of the USSR.

United Nations (UN): an international organization founded in 1945, after the World War II and intended to promote peace, security, and cooperation. China now not only belongs to the UN but is also a permanent member of its most powerful body, the Security Council.

Vietnam War: the war between Communist North Vietnam and noncommunist South Vietnam that lasted from 1954 to 1975. American troops fought alongside the South Vietnamese from 1964 until 1973. China backed North Vietnam by providing ammunition and weapons.

World War I: the major war fought between 1914 and 1918. The main opponents were the Central Powers (Germany, Austria-Hungary, and Turkey) and the Allies (Britain, France, Russia, and the United States). China and Japan also fought on the side of the Allies, who won the war in November 1918.

World War II: the major war fought between 1939 and 1945. The main opponents were the Axis Powers (Germany, Italy, and Japan) and the Allies (Britain, France, the Soviet Union, and the United States). During this war, Japan invaded and occupied much of northern and eastern China.

INDEX